ON
FENNER'S
SWARD

A History of Cambridge University
Cricket Club

ON
FENNER'S
SWARD

*A History of Cambridge University
Cricket Club*

GILES PHILLIPS

To Peter

Best wishes

Giles Phillips

TEMPUS

First published 2005

Tempus Publishing Limited
The Mill, Brimscombe Port,
Stroud, Gloucestershire, GL5 2QG
www.tempus-publishing.com

© Giles Phillips, 2005

British Library Cataloguing in Publication Data.
A catalogue record for this book is available from the British Library.

ISBN 0 7524 3412 8

Typesetting and origination by Tempus Publishing Limited
Printed in Great Britain

CONTENTS

FOREWORD

It was during the summer of 1956 that I took my first casual steps towards becoming a first-class cricketer. I say casual because at the time I was more concerned with developing my golf swing and worrying about exams, and had no intention of playing cricket in the foreseeable future. Yet in no time at all, I had obtained a permanent place in the University eleven. My brother John was responsible for this remarkable change in my fortunes, for it was he who put my name forward for freshmen's nets. One thing led to another, and after a good showing in two trial games I was picked for the first three games against the might of Surrey, Yorkshire and Lancashire. Although I made three ducks, I also made three forties, enough to retain my place for good.

After such a tough baptism, I was convinced of the need to take the game seriously, which is precisely what I did from then on. I was taken under the wing of Cyril Coote, groundsman and mentor to many generations of Cambridge cricketers. I began to realise what a great opportunity I had been given to learn the game on Cyril's perfect wickets, and how important a contribution Cambridge University Cricket Club has made to the game over a period of nearly 200 years. I am convinced that, like many others before and since, I was able to make my mark on the game far more quickly at Cambridge than I would have done for a county, especially when I was given the responsibility of being captain in 1958.

The Cambridge team of my time was able to call on such great players as Bob Barber, Roger Prideaux, Ossie Wheatley and Gamini Goonesena, and while Fenner's is not the breeding-ground it once was, the talent is still there if only admissions tutors can see the benefits that sporting excellence can bring to the University. I welcome this long overdue celebration of all that is good about the Club, and hope that its publication will be a timely reminder of how much poorer the world would be without the timeless sound of leather on willow at Fenner's in the Spring.

Ted Dexter

Ted Dexter

INTRODUCTION

When I first came to live in Cambridge in 1990, I saw Fenner's as a great place to spend an afternoon watching some first-class cricket for free, with perhaps the bonus of seeing a famous face or two thrown in for good measure. Little did I think then that the fortunes of the University Cricket Club would become so important to me. It was only when I came back to Cambridge as a postgraduate student in 1998 that I began to identify with what had become my team. It helped that I knew one of that year's eleven, Ken Walker, and that he played a memorable innings for our college in a famous win against the mighty Trinity. I even batted with him for a while, and realised what a tremendous privilege it was to be part of a community that included so many talented men and women in so many different fields, including sport. It also brought home to me just how good a cricketer you have to be to obtain your Blue, even if not everyone in the squad may be quite first-class standard. In short, I was hooked, and I wanted to know more about the ghosts of Fenner's' past, present and future.

That's all very nice, you may be thinking, but why drag us into it? Why another book about CUCC? Well, admittedly there have been a couple of books in recent years, but they covered the Varsity Match, one of them almost solely in pictures. In fact, there has not been a history of the Club since 1902, and an awful lot has happened in the last century besides the annual clash with Oxford. I thought it was high time that the story was updated, especially when there has been so much upheaval in the last few years. So, in writing this book, I wanted both to celebrate a great tradition and take stock of the Club's current situation. While fervently hoping that it remains a force to be reckoned with, it seemed important to record the dramas of the past before they are forgotten. At the time of writing it is also 250 years since the University played its first recorded game of cricket, giving a final justification for the timing of this volume. I can only hope that its contents prove worthy of the countless illustrious names that have adorned the cricket fields of Cambridge over that period.

On a final note of self-indulgence, I still feel, despite the modern obsession with meaningless lists of trivia, that there is room for the selection of a 'best ever' eleven, as long as the task hasn't been performed in public for a decent period of time. As far as I am aware, a 'best ever' Cambridge team has not appeared in print for over fifty years, so, in order to bring matters up to date, here is mine in batting order:

Majid Khan
David Sheppard
Peter May
Hubert Ashton
Kumor Shri Duleepsinhji
Stanley Jackson (Captain)
Allan Steel
Sammy Woods
Gregor MacGregor (Wicketkeeper)
Ken Farnes
Charles Marriott

Of course, I fully expect a vitriolic response to my selections, given that I have left out some of the all-time greats such as Ranji and Jessop, but all I can say is that I have picked the team purely on impact and achievement *at Cambridge*. Hence no room for those two, or others who played their best cricket in later life. Clearly, one could choose another eleven players almost equally good, but a decision had to be made, and I have to stand by it. I leave you, dear reader, to make up your own mind.

This book could not have been completed without help from many different sources, and in particular I must thank: Don Ambrose, Joe Arnold, Peter Batten, David Beaumont, Holly Bennion, David Birks, Rob Boddie, Professor David Buckingham CBE, Ramsay Cox, John Dewes, Ted Dexter, Hubert Doggart, Hugh Faulkner, Michael Foley, Colin Grant, Stephen Green, David Hallett, Keith Hayhurst, Roger Heavens, Dr Andrew Hignell, James Howarth, Dr Anthony Hyde, Doug Insole, Gron Jones, Gordon Mckinna, Frank Maskell MBE, Shaun Mundy, Dr Mark Nicholls, Jim Parsons, Philip Paine, Chris Scott, Professor Ken Siddle, Geoff Stedall, Willie Sugg, Richard Turner, Malcolm White, Kate Wiseman and the late Michael Wolton. My friends and family, especially my parents, gave me support and encouragement throughout, and finally a special thank you to Elena, who provided more inspiration than she knows. My sincere apologies to anyone I have inadvertently left out.

In addition to those already acknowledged, the following kindly gave permission for illustrations to be reproduced: Bodyline Books, Cambridge Central Library and the Cambridgeshire Collection, *Cambridge Evening News*, Cambridge University Cricket Club, Patrick Eagar, Glamorgan County Cricket Club, Paul Harrison, Lancashire County Cricket Club, MCC, Press Association Photos, Adrian Shankar, Grenville Simons, Somerset County Cricket Club, Sussex County Cricket Club, and Lewis Todd (Cambridge market). I have made every effort to trace copyright holders, and would welcome the chance to correct any omissions in this regard.

ONE

THE FIRST GREEN SHOOTS

A scholar travelling forward in time from the Middle Ages would have had no difficulty recognising Cambridge in the seventeenth century: dunghills in the streets, dead animals choking the watercourses and a cheerful disregard for sanitary regulations by students and townsfolk alike. Only in 1614 did Hobson's famous fountain bring fresh water to the centre of town. Outbreaks of plague were frequent, and students were blamed for bringing it in from outside. Since they also left town at the end of each term, there was some resentment that they could often avoid catching it, simply by being elsewhere, a luxury not available to residents. In 1630, however, there was such a virulent and long-lasting attack that all people were affected equally, and through sheer humanity town and gown were forced to pull together.

Cambridge was beginning to grow, however. The population in the 1660s had risen to 6,000, an increase of twenty per cent compared with Elizabeth I's reign. Student numbers were also rising: in 1619, there were 509 matriculants for the whole University, a figure not matched (apart from the post-plague years of 1631 and 1667) until 1864. A decline in student numbers set in later in the century, as students who wanted to become members of the clergy started to disappear. At this time, Cambridge University was more or less a seminary for the Church of England, so the draining away of this source of students meant radical action was required. The first signs of an attempt to make Cambridge a genuine seat of learning came with the appointment of Isaac Barrow to the new Lucasian Chair of Mathematics in 1660.

With all the emphasis on the moral improvement of scholars, entertainment was rather thin on the ground. The University's Elizabethan Statutes forbade:

dice and (except at Christmas) cards: daily resorting to the town: vain clubbing of money: sword-playing, fencing and dancing schools: gaming-houses: cockfighting, bear or bull-baiting: quoits: or looking at any of these.

Oxford University picked up on the same theme in its Laudian Statutes of 1636. F.W. Newman, in his 1843 translation of Huber's *The English Universities*, inserts a note referring to Title XV of the statutes, *de Moribus Conformandis* ('Of Forming the Manners'). He quotes it as saying that prohibited games included 'every kind of game in which money is concerned, such as dibs, cards, cricketing in the private grounds or gardens of townspeople'.

Is this the first reference to cricket at either of the Universities, and by implication a sign that the game was already established at Cambridge? Alas, it appears not. The original statutes were in Latin, and G.R.M. Ward, in his official translation published two years later, refers to 'ball-play' instead of cricket, which is a far more likely interpretation, and one that admits of many possibilities. While 'ball-play' may well include cricket, there is no evidence to suggest that the statute is being specific, and it seems most likely that Newman was temporarily struck down by a severe bout of that well-known ailment, Victorian sentimentalism.

The penalties for the misdemeanours mentioned in the statute were not trifling; to undergraduates, 'corporal chastisement' was offered, while graduates were fined six shillings and eight pence. There was also a fine of:

twenty shillings to those who take in such gamesters, and of imprisonment to boot, until they put in security to harbour such gamblers no more.

Little wonder, then, that cricket does not seem to have gained a real foothold at the University during the seventeenth century. It is difficult to believe, though, that the game was unheard of there. References during the century seem to place the game's origins in The Weald, and many of the sons of the wealthy in the area were educated at one of the four top schools, Eton, Harrow, Winchester and Westminster. Since it is known that cricket was played at these schools in the 1600s (although inter-school matches started much later), it is no great leap of the imagination to surmise that the alumni of these establishments took the game with them to Cambridge. Indeed, Henry Cuffen, who took a BA at King's College in 1623–4, was still playing cricket in 1629. By this time he was curate of Ruckinge in Kent, and we are told that he was brought before the Archdeacon's Court for 'playing at Cricketts' immediately after evening prayers.

So cricket clearly was being played, in some shape or form, at the University in this period, but was not yet anything like as popular as the officially sanctioned games of tennis (what we would now call Real Tennis) and bowls. Of the sixteen colleges standing at the time, nine had tennis courts, thirteen had bowling greens and eight had both. Even then, students were heavily restricted as to when they could play. At Emmanuel College in 1651, the tennis court was kept locked, and no play was allowed between 1 and 3 p.m., and from 8 p.m. to 10 a.m. The exception was if a fellow wanted to play, and he would have been allowed to bring along a fellow-commoner.

The fellow-commoner was a strange species of student, but one who was to have a big part to play in our story. His key privilege was to be allowed to sit at the same table as the fellows, but not only that, he could say more or less what he liked to them. He could also do what he liked, as he was invariably an heir to a great estate, and if a Cambridge academic wanted to keep his easy living he had to know which side his bread was buttered. Therefore fellow-commoners were excused from regulations and tutorials, and instead went hunting, played tennis, or recovered from a night's carousing. As the century progressed, it became clear that cricket could be added to the list of diversions.

By the turn of the century, students of this ilk were helping to make the game an increasingly popular pastime, whether or not money was changing hands. In 1706, William Goldwin, a graduate of King's the previous year, was ordained a deacon in London, and wrote the first real poem on cricket, *In Certamen Pilae* ('On a Game of Ball'), mock-epic in style and running to ninety-five lines. As with the statutes, the verses are in Latin, so cricket is never referred to directly by name. The description given nevertheless makes it abundantly clear which sport Goldwin is eulogising:

> The word is given, and, urged with might,
> speeds the greased ball in level flight,
> and o'er the grassy surface sweeps;
> with bended knee the batsman keeps
> a forward stance, to watch its way.

And so it continues. Aside from the reminder that bowling was underarm at this stage in the game's evolution, we have a picture which is still recognisable three centuries later, and that surely must have been based on the author's very fresh memories of playing and watching the game himself during his time at Cambridge. We can indulge Goldwin's idyllic view of cricket if we remember that it was surely in tune with his overall perception of his student days.

Goldwin's contemporaries clearly shared his enthusiasm for the game, and by 1710 it had finally come to the notice of the authorities, though by now the attitude to cricket and other sports had mellowed. Writing in a pamphlet published that year, Thomas Blomer, a Fellow of Trinity College, records the general distaste at the appointment of a St John's man, Richard Bentley, as the new Master. Bentley further incurred the wrath of Blomer's colleagues by giving permission for the undergraduates to leave Hall before Grace had been said, while the Fellows had to remain. His reasoning was that students:

dispatch their meals with greater expedition than the Fellows do (and)... wax impatient to run home to their studies, others to try a fair fall upon the grass, and others to make a match at football or cricket.

How little the mealtime habits of the young have changed, and how important a reminder that university sport has always relied upon the altruism of academic staff. Finally, then, we have the first solid, direct reference to cricket being played at the

University, and now the trickle of references becomes a gently meandering stream for the rest of the century.

The powers that be may not have wanted a total ban on entertainment, but students were still in Cambridge to be educated. Christopher Wordsworth, writing in the last quarter of the nineteenth century, refers to Regulation XVIII, which, he says, had been issued frequently since at least 1714. It forbade undergraduates to visit 'a coffee-house, tennis-court, cricket-ground etc. between 9 and 12 a.m.' (the hours of lectures). Confusingly, Wordsworth later mentions the same regulation as dating from 1750, with a fine of ten shillings for each transgression, but the gist is clear – cricket was merely an amusement, and not an activity that could be allowed to stand in the way of the serious business of life.

A clear illustration of this attitude comes from the 1740s, in the person of Henry Venn, who left Jesus College in 1745 with something of a reputation:

He was extremely fond of cricket, and reckoned one of the best players in the University. In the week before he was ordained [June 1747], he played in a match between Surrey and All England: the match had excited considerable interest, and was attended by a very numerous body of spectators. When the game terminated, in favour of the side on which he played, he threw down his bat, saying, 'Whoever wants a bat, which has done me good service, may take that, as I have no further occasion for it.' His friends inquiring the reason, he replied, 'Because I am to be ordained on Sunday; and I will never have it said of me, "Well struck, Parson!"'

Venn was true to his word – he is not heard of again on the cricket field, but he did become a leading figure in the Church.

Inevitably, despite being put into perspective by the demands of the scholastic world, cricket and other sports became more organised as the century advanced. The *Public Advertiser* of 10 June 1755, besides advertising Samuel Johnson's forthcoming *Dictionary of the English Language*, and reporting on an unsuccessful attempt to rob a post-boy in Cambridge, has the following:

Tuesday and Thursday last [June 3rd and 5th] two matches of Cricket were played betwixt the Gentlemen of Eton and the Gentlemen of this University, which were both decided in favour of the latter. The Gentlemen of the University won as easily this year as the Gentlemen of Eton did the last.

So we have the University's first recorded loss in 1754, and the first win a year later. Was the opposition really Eton, or in fact old boys up at the University? Obviously, by now the link between the two was firmly entrenched, so it would be perfectly reasonable for such a fixture to take place, given the relatively short journey. Also, there are references to several matches between Eton and All England in Newmarket in 1751. Again, though, reports are not totally unequivocal as to whether the team represented past or present schoolboys. Furthermore, as far as can be gathered, Eton did not start playing Harrow until the early 1800s. Also, it was clearly common for games of various kinds to be played at the Universities between undergraduates from different schools. Writing on 4 June 1760 about Oxford, the Reverend James Woodforde records:

The Eaton and Winchester People plaid at Crickett against the whole University eleven on each side and the latter were shamefully beat off the field.

On balance, it would seem that Cambridge's game was of a similar stamp. However that may be, there was no doubt that the walls had finally been battered down and competitive cricket had arrived.

Where were these games played? We are given a clue by a reference to a game between Cambridge (Town) and Saffron Walden in 1757. This took place on Jesus Green, to the immediate north of the college, and this is one of two likely locations for the University's match. Jesus was the first college to have its own cricket ground, but there is no evidence to suggest it had one as early as this, despite the following memoir of Gilbert Wakefield, admitted to Jesus in 1772:

in the spring of the year... I was so enamoured of rambling in the open air, through solitary fields, or by a river's side, of cricket and of fishing.

An early view of the chaotic scenes on Parker's Piece.

Although the official history of the college calls this the first reference to cricket at Jesus, it is so vague that there can be no certainty about where Wakefield played cricket. The other strong possibility is Parker's Piece, already a popular resort for townspeople and students alike.

Although we have no evidence as to exactly where these matches took place, it is tempting to hazard a guess at the name of one of the participants: Charles Powlett, eldest son of Charles, 3rd Duke of Bolton, left Trinity College in 1755, and must have been a keen cricketer at Cambridge. Later in life, he was a key figure in establishing the fame of the Hambledon Club in Hampshire, and was also one of the committee that revised the Laws of Cricket at the Star and Garter in Pall Mall in 1774. He was exactly the sort of rich student with the time and the inclination to devote to such occasions, and there were to be many more like him as the nineteenth century dawned.

TWO

A CLUB IS BORN

On Friday last a grand match at cricket was played on Parker's Piece between eleven gentlemen of King's College and eleven gentlemen of the rest of the university, which was won by the former, with five wickets to go down.

UNIVERSITY		KING'S COLLEGE	
1st Innings	*131*	*1st Innings*	*116*
2nd ditto	*187*	*2nd ditto*	*202*
318		*318*	
		and five wickets to go down	

This is the second time the gentlemen of King's College have beaten the university this season.

So says the *Cambridge Chronicle* of Friday 30 May 1817, and however strange the mathematics may be, it was a clear demonstration of the continuing influence of King's men on University cricket. Its strength lay in the fact that Etonians normally ended up there, Eton and King's being the twin foundations of Henry VI. This match seems to have become a regular fixture around this time, as there were five games between 1816 and 1820, but there was something special about this particular occasion. It turned out to be a warm-up for what is now regarded as Cambridge University's first ever 'first-class' fixture. The *Cambridge Chronicle* of 6 June takes up the story:

A cricket match was played on Parker's Piece last Friday [May 30], between eleven gentlemen of the university (including King's College) and eleven members of the cricket club of this town, which was won by the former, by a majority of 37 runs.

UNIVERSITY		TOWN	
1st Innings	128	1st Innings	91
2nd ditto	76	2nd ditto	76
	204		167

Unfortunately, that is the only detail we have on the game, a successful debut by the University, and one that began a long-running series between 'Town and Gown'. The scoring, unlike the King's game, was about average for the time. Pitches would not be scarified or rolled for many years to come, and batting was always something of a lottery. The score of over 200 to win by King's was thus an exceptional effort.

This was a good time for the growth of cricket, after many fallow years. England was emerging from a long period of social hardship, exacerbated by the Enclosure Acts, and a twenty-three-year war with France. It was just two years since Napoleon's defeat at Waterloo, and cricket was feeling its way again after a quarter of a century of neglect. Cambridge was lucky to have retained much of its common land, and its undergraduates were ready to make maximum use of the opportunities this presented. University cricket was about to come of age.

The Club was started probably in 1824–5 by, and managed by, three Etonians of equal rank, whatever they were called, of whom I was one. The first match recorded will be found in Lillywhite's Scores as played in April 1825 on the New Ground at Cambridge.

These are the reminiscences of Herbert Jenner, as told to William Justice Ford, the club's first historian, seventy-five years later. While we are indebted to Jenner's memory for much detail of these early days, it appears to be faulty in this instance. Though information about the foundation of the Club is frustratingly scant, we are at least blessed with the first scorebook, and this contradicts Jenner's version of events. 'The University Cricket Club Instituted AD 1820' is confidently asserted on its grubby green front cover, and although when we turn to page one, the inscription 'inst? 1820' introduces an element of doubt, it seems to imply only that there is the possibility of an earlier date.

As far as the compilers of this scorebook were aware the first treasurers were H. Hannington and C. Oxenden, joined in 1821 by P. Gurdon. Their roles were presumably equivalent to president, secretary and treasurer, and, in the absence of any evidence to the contrary, we have to assume that Hannington and Oxenden were responsible for founding the Club. Exactly how this came about we will never know, as the original minute book has long been lost. We do at least have the original membership list on page three of the book, annotated at a later date. There were forty-two members on the list (one of them later crossed out), sixteen of them honorary, including Lord Grey of Trinity. Indeed, the nine members from Trinity represented the most from any College. Page two explains that:

*Herbert Jenner captained Cambridge in the first ever
Varsity Match.*

*No member becomes 'honorary' unless he continues a member of the UCC until he shall have
left the University or graduated.*

Respectability was clearly important to the Club, and lack of it did not go
unpunished:

*In consequence of the bad conduct and incivility of Sterne towards some of the members of the
Club in 1820: Be it remembered that (by the vote of the Club) he is never to be suffered to
play in any match against the said Club.*

The Club proved as good as its word. Apparently, as reported in the local press, the
offence was caused by Sterne telling a six-foot 'gownsman' that he would 'lick' him.
Two years later, his brother was picked for the Town team against the University, but
the students refused to let him play. The Town club seems meekly to have acquiesced,
much to the chagrin of the press, which saw it as an inglorious episode in the history
of both clubs.

On the playing side, the book gives details of no less than seven practice matches in
1820, including an intriguing one between the 'Hs and Cs' and the 'Rest', won by the
former by five wickets, despite 66 by Oxenden. His fellow Treasurer scored 68 out of
137 in his side's first innings. There was also a chance for King's to give the University
its annual beating, although this time it won by only one wicket in a tight finish.
Finally, there were the most important games of the season, against Cambridge Town.
There were in fact two, but only one is recorded in the scorebook – a loss by 77 runs
(although the scorer seems to have miscalculated the University's second innings total).

Perhaps the University was handicapped by not having the King's men in either game, but in the second it was lucky to have any players at all. The game descended into farce when the University, following-on 170 behind, had to forfeit the match when several players suddenly left town. There was nothing unusual at the time in this casual attitude, but it did mean that playing standards improved only gradually.

Membership was on the up, however, rising to seventy-four in 1822, even though, according to the scorebook, 'owing to the exceptionally cold and wet season there were very few days which were at all calculated for cricket' in 1821. There were in addition three dons who subscribed a guinea and had the 'privilege of the tent'. There was also a success to celebrate on the pitch that year, the Town being beaten by seven wickets, with George Hume scoring 44 not out to go with his 97 not out in 1821. This was the last first-class match he ever played, so he retired with the happy average of 82.5. Regrettably, the scorebook suddenly ends there, and there is no record of any more encounters with the Town until 1825, the year Jenner made his debut for the club and became treasurer.

The scorebook also makes an intriguing reference to the 'New' ground belonging to the University, on which the Club played first against the Town on 24 May 1821. Jenner describes the ground in Ford's book as an:

enclosed field of eight acres, near a newly built chapel in the parish of Barnwell, for which we paid £30 a year. After a couple of years two acres were taken off to increase the burial-ground: rent, however, remained the same. Under such circumstances it was not to be expected that we could play many matches.

Baker's 1837 map of Cambridge clearly shows the ground and the new church to the north of Mill Road, about 300 yards north-east of what is now Fenner's. The whole site is now dedicated to Mill Road Cemetery, a tranquil and beautiful site overlooked by one of Anglia Polytechnic University's less pleasing building blocks; a delicious irony considering the events to be described later in our story. The front of the keeper's cottage still bears the inscription 'Consecrated Nov 7 1848', giving the cricket ground a maximum lifespan of about twenty years. It seems that in fact the University stopped using it as early as 1830, as there are no references to games played there after that date.

Another description of the ground has emerged from a court transcript of a sexual assault of 1823. It was apparently approached by a high-hedged road twenty-two feet wide, and surrounded by a fence with a high gate. The map that went with the transcript shows a shed in the north-west corner of the ground, used by the workmen who tended it. Clearly the Club was already employing staff, perhaps as bowlers to give the students practice, in addition to their work as groundsmen.

According to Jenner, cricket was still not very popular, a fact that was not helped by the location of the ground:

We played at some distance from the colleges, and there were no tents, or flags to show that a match was going on.

Above: *The keeper's cottage at the site of the Club's first ground.*

Right: *A plan of the ground from an 1823 court case.*

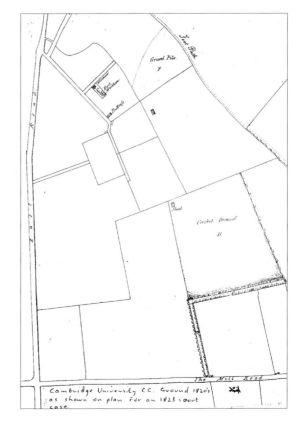

The 'tent' referred to in the scorebook in 1822 must therefore have been on Parker's Piece, even though Jenner claimed the University never played there. Indeed, Ford's book shows an engraving of undergraduates on the Piece in 1842, with dons sitting in a marquee that is remarkably close to the action. Jenner's memory is clearly at fault, as the annual Town game was often played on Parker's Piece during his time. There was definitely interest in these clashes as the main fixtures of the year, even if games at the Barnwell site were sparsely attended.

The scorebook of 1820–22, and the subsequent match book, are very evocative documents, but the bare figures give no clue as to the personalities of the 1820s. For instance, it would be fascinating to know more about Charles Chapman, the first man to carry his bat through a completed innings for the University when he finished undefeated with 47 out of a total of 90 in a convincing win over the Town in 1826. Alas, such figures are condemned to remain ever shadowy, with the one notable exception of Jenner himself. Born Herbert Jenner in 1806, he changed his name to Jenner-Fust in 1864, and survived the reign of Queen Victoria, before finally dying in 1904. A true cricketing all-rounder, he was one of the great wicketkeepers of his time, and would often bowl at one end and keep wicket at the other. This did not present any problems, as there was no time wasted donning protective gear:

I kept wicket without pads or gloves; in fact, pads were not heard of in my young days, and the player would have been laughed at who tried to protect his shins. Knee-breeches, and thin gauze silk stockings, doubled up at the ankles, formed a popular costume.

R.J.P. Broughton, a Blue in the 1830s, who saw Jenner play after the latter had left Cambridge, attested to his immense agility, describing him as 'virtually wicketkeeper, short slip and short leg'.

Jenner's most significant role in the Club's history was not so much as a player, but in the part he played in setting up what has become the longest-running series of matches in first-class cricket: the Varsity Match. Regrettably, he deserves less of the credit for this than he seemed to think; in Ford's book, he claims to have issued the challenge to Oxford, but in reality it was exactly the other way round. Charles Wordsworth, nephew of the poet and later Bishop of St Andrews, wrote about it at some length for the 'Cricket' volume of the Badminton Library in 1888:

In the newly published Life of my younger brother Christopher, the late Bishop of Lincoln, the following words are to be found, quoted from his private journal: – 'Friday' (no date – but early in June 1826). 'Heard from Charles. He wishes that Oxford and Cambridge play a match at cricket'. … Having played against Eton for four years, from… 1822 to 1825… I had a large acquaintance among cricketers who had gone off from those schools and from Harrow to both Universities. … Nothing came of my wish to bring about a match between the Universities in 1826. But in 1827 the proposal was carried into effect. Though an Oxford man, my home was at Cambridge, my father being Master of Trinity; and this gave me opportunities for communicating with men of that University, many of whom remained up for the vacations…

I remember calling upon Barnard of King's, who had been captain of an Eton Eleven against whom I had played, and who was now one of the foremost Cambridge cricketers, and he gave me reason to fear that no King's man would be able to play at the time proposed (early in June), though that time would be within the Cambridge vacation and not within ours, because their men, at King's, were kept up longer than at the other Colleges. ... In those ante-railway days it was necessary to get permission from the College authorities to go up to London in term time, and the permission was not readily granted... in order to gain my end, I had to present myself to the Dean and tell him that I wished to be allowed to go to London – not to play a game of cricket (that would not have been listened to) – but to consult a dentist; a piece of Jesuitry which was understood, I believe, equally well on both sides.

So, Wordsworth, who was also responsible for founding the Boat Race in 1829, was the instigator of the annual cricket match against Cambridge. As it turned out, there was indeed only one King's man in the team put out by Cambridge, although there were no less than eight Etonians. The man who accepted the invitation was not Barnard but Jenner himself, relishing the chance to resume hostilities against an old adversary. In the Eton *v.* Harrow matches of 1822 and 1823, Wordsworth had bowled him three times for 2, 0 and 7 respectively, so there were some old scores to settle. Wordsworth must have had other connections in high places, for he managed to persuade Benjamin Aislabie, another ex-Etonian and secretary of the MCC, to allow the match to be played at Lord's. This was on Thomas Lord's third site, open since 1814, and still the home of cricket today.

   As with every other aspect of this first match, there is some uncertainty about when it was actually played. The confusion arises because of two announcements in the weekly journal *Bell's Life*. The first, dated Sunday 3 June 1827 states:

A Grand Match at cricket will be played tomorrow in Lord's Cricket Ground, between the resident Members of the two Universities of Cambridge and Oxford.

A week later, on 10 June, it records:

Owing to the unfavourable state of the weather last Monday, the match between Oxford and Cambridge was postponed to a future day.

For all we know from *Bell's Life*, that 'future day' never came about, since it makes no further reference to the match. But assuredly the match did take place, and we have to return to Wordsworth for a more authoritative, if rather tentative view on the date:

I can only say that I do not remember any postponement, as I think I should do had such been the case; and what is more, 'a few days' later would have brought it within our vacation, and so would have rendered my piece of Jesuitism unnecessary.

As it is, the match is commonly regarded as having taken place on 4 and 5 June, with one day washed out, presumably the Monday if *Bell's Life* is correct. Since the newspapers virtually ignored the occasion, the match may well have taken place the next day without the press being aware of it.

Cambridge would have been grateful for the curtailment of the match due to the inclement weather, for Wordworth's team, taking first strike, ran up the unusually high total of 258. The legendary William Webb Ellis, 'inventor' of rugby, scored only 12 batting at number three, but R. Price held the innings together, top-scoring with 71. The only consolation for Jenner was that he managed to bowl his old rival for 8, and also took at least four more wickets. It is difficult to be certain, since scorecards of the time only credit the bowler with a wicket if he bowled a batsman, or had him lbw; catches and stumpings were credited to the fielder alone. The Lord's wickets of the time were notoriously treacherous, the grass being kept down by bringing sheep on to the ground a day or two before the match, so Webb and Kingdon faced an uphill task when they went out to open the innings for Cambridge.

1827 is also notable in cricket history for a series of matches set up by the MCC to test out the new-fangled round-arm bowling. Those who advocated the new method were called the 'March of Intellect', a trendy term at the time denoting belief in progress or, if you happened to be a reactionary, antipathy to anything novel. The matches showed that cricket would not be ruined by what some regarded as 'throwing', and in 1835 the legislators bowed to the inevitable and allowed the arm to be raised to shoulder height. None of the gentlemanly exponents in the Varsity Match would have been troubled by the controversy, as they continued to bowl underarm throughout. Indeed, given the helpful pitch, no innovation was required by the bowlers, as Wordsworth relates:

the state of the ground being in my favour, I was singularly successful with my left-hand twist from the off, bringing down no less than seven wickets in the one innings for only 25 runs. Jenner… was the only batsman who made any stand against it. He had learnt by painful experience how to deal with it.

Jenner top-scored with 47, the next highest score being Romilly's 8 in a total of 92. Wordsworth must have kept his own record of his bowling analysis, since such details were not included in scorebooks at the time.

Before moving on, one other Cambridge name merits a special mention. Edward Horsman batted number eleven and took a couple of wickets, and played again in the 1829 Varsity Match, but after that he does not feature in the chronicles of cricket. He resurfaces as an MP in the 1830s, and in 1840, according to J.D. Betham:

as the result of a bitter correspondence, in which he accused James Bradshaw, MP for Canterbury, of secretly sympathising with the Chartists, and of speaking disrespectfully of the Queen, a duel was fought at Wormwood Scrubs, but without injury to either party.

Horsman survived intact, and rose to be Irish Secretary in the 1850s.

So, the first Varsity Match ended with a draw very much in Oxford's favour, a balance of power that fortunately shifted towards Cambridge in future contests. Apart from another rain-ruined game in 1844, it turned out to be the only undecided match in the series until 1888. There were many tussles to be lost and won before then.

THREE

TOWN *v.* GOWN

1828 was a quiet year for the club, with only one game being recorded. This was a very close encounter with the Town side, resulting in a victory for the students by a mere 10 runs. The University was 3 runs behind on the first innings, but was rescued by the captain, Edward Pickering of Eton and St John's, who made a gallant 44 not out in the second innings, in addition to taking ten wickets in the match. The Town team found the target of 121 just too much in the face of the University's superior bowling.

Pickering, like so many graduates at the time, returned to his alma mater on going down from Cambridge, and indeed taught there for the rest of his life, being buried in the school chapel in 1852. He retained the captaincy in 1829, and masterminded another victory against the Town in an even more extraordinary game. This time 'gown' managed just 77 in the first innings, and trailed by 63. However, Pickering led a resurgence with 72 not out, leaving a tricky 190 to win and the Town fell just 3 runs short in another thrilling finish.

The team was thus in good spirits when it set out for Oxford at the beginning of June. Lord's was seemingly not available, so the ground of the Magdalen Club, on Cowley Common, was given over to the second University Match. A picture of what the Common, and indeed Parker's Piece, must have been like, is given by James Pycroft, writing in 1886, about his student days at Oxford in the 1830s:

On the Magdalen ground we used to practise with six wickets along the upper side, facing at a distance of about fifty yards, six along the lower side. Here we had twelve men batting and twelve men between the rows bowling…

With the common also being a popular area for equestrian exercise, the state of the outfield can be imagined, but Parker's Piece must have been even worse, as

Cambridge was not regarded as fit to stage the Varsity Match in those early days. Indeed, Fenner's finally played host to the fixture for the first time in the twenty-first century. One can further picture the scene through Pycroft's description of the sidelines:

We had no pavilion, only a long tent for dinner under the victualling of a very remarkable man – a man who might have made a fortune at Oxford with common prudence, so popular was he and so well did he understand University men – 'Old King Cole'. Few men will ever forget Cole's portly figure, his watch chain and seals plumbing a perpendicular clear of his toes, standing before the tent…

A letter from Charles Wordsworth to Charles Merivale, a fellow ex-Harrovian up at Cambridge, gives a tantalising glimpse of the *ad hoc* nature of the match's organisation. After listing Oxford's team for the game, he goes on to say:

This information is for Pickering, if you will be kind enough to forward it to him, and to thank him for his letter. Ask him if we are to do anything about an umpire. Ashby stands by for us. Printed bills will reach Cambridge in a day or two.

We will never know whether Cambridge did bring its own umpire, or what were the contents of Pickering's letter, but it does show the extent to which the staging of the match relied on both captains, even down to the production of publicity materials (regrettably none of them seems to have survived).

However much the game was advertised, it received scant attention in the press, especially when compared to the space devoted to the first Boat Race. This took place at Henley on 10 June, in front of a crowd estimated at 20,000. Oxford won easily, thanks partly to the skills of Wordsworth himself. In another letter, published in the magazine *Cricket* in 1887, he explains the effect of the two contests being only two days apart:

I was invited… to make one of our Oxford crew. I did not like to refuse, though this involved giving up cricket for that year, and I offered to withdraw my name from the Eleven; but I was pressed not to do so… I was suffering from an imposthume (a posteriori, the result of stricter diet in training for the boat)… which troubled me so that I could scarcely stand upright when I went to the wicket.

A swelling in an unnamed part of the body would seem to be a poor excuse for making a pair, as Wordsworth proceeded to do. However, he would have been little concerned at this misfortune, as he became the first victorious captain in the series; Oxford trounced the other place by 115 runs in quite a low-scoring contest. Wordsworth was again bowled in the first innings by Jenner, but the perpetrator was not Herbert but his younger brother Charles. The latter emulated his sibling by taking five wickets, and keeping wicket at the other end for good measure. His performance was the only one of any merit for Cambridge, even Pickering's powers of recovery deserting him on the big occasion.

Pycroft relates that Cole was also a moneylender and bookmaker of sorts; during the match:

Cole met a similar character and an equally important supporter on the Cambridge side – boasting in the most confident manner of his 'gentlemen'. 'Well,' said Cole, 'you seem to make so certain, but I'd take odds that two of our bats make more in one innings than all your eleven put together.' 'Done for £10 to £1.'

Although strictly, given the actual scores, Cole could not have won the bet, the message was clear: Oxford had the sort of supporter who was not to be trifled with!

Support for the game in Cambridge was fairly thin on the ground at the start of the 1830s, and few undergraduates of any calibre stepped forward to make their name. One who did make a lasting mark on the game was the Honourable Frederick Ponsonby, of Harrow and Trinity College, who later became one of the founders of the legendary wandering club I Zingari and a prime mover in the establishment of Surrey County Cricket Club. The only major fixture until 1835 remained the Town game, won five times in a row by the latter, until the sequence was broken in 1833, albeit by a student team augmented by two local professionals.

Things began to pick up in 1835, the year when round-arm bowling was finally legalised. Cambridge played the MCC for the first time, and was granted a return match at Lord's during the holidays. Although both games were lost by large margins, it showed that University cricket was beginning to be taken seriously by the authorities. This growing reputation was further enhanced in 1836 by the simultaneous emergence of two of the early greats of Cambridge cricket, Charles Taylor and John Kirwan.

Taylor was regarded as the finest amateur batsman of the day, and later had a long career with Sussex. Elegant but effective, he managed to average 18 with the bat for the University, at a time when double-figure scores were considered respectable. William Glover, a Cambridge don who wrote his memoirs half a century later, described him as:

a kind of gentleman Pilch (Fuller Pilch was the leading professional batsman of the time), *with much of his style, to the 'off'. But, by placing his legs apart, and resting equally on both, he could rarely turn in time for a 'leg-ball'; in fact, during several years, I scarcely ever saw him make a good 'leg' hit.*

He was also an early example of the Cambridge cricketer who excelled at nearly everything he tried. Robert Broughton, in the eleven with Taylor that year, tells us that they once played tennis together, with Taylor using a ginger-beer bottle instead of a racket, and furthermore:

C. G. Taylor was considered the best amateur batsman of his day.

Taylor bet a friend of mine that he would himself make a pair of trousers and wear them on the King's Parade at Cambridge. He won his bet, and nobody would have guessed that the things were not made by a professional person. At another time he made a bet that he would learn to play the piano and sing in six weeks, and he did it.

Kirwan, on the other hand, was one of the most fearsome fast bowlers of the 1830s, and took no less than 101 wickets for Cambridge in only fifteen games, becoming the first to pass the century for either University. However, as soon as he graduated he was lost to serious cricket, dedicating himself to the Church like so many of his contemporaries. Pycroft, who opened for Oxford in the Varsity Match that year, described him thus:

Kirwan was the swiftest underhand (either a sling or a jerk) of his day. In the then state of Lord's, we could not have stood against him.

After a tremendous start to the season, in which the Town and the MCC were beaten on Parker's Piece (Kirwan taking fifteen wickets against the Town, and Broughton hitting 8 off one delivery in the second game), Kirwan suddenly became unavailable. Whether this was through injury is not recorded, but it left the attack looking rather threadbare for the two games that followed at Lord's. First, MCC gained revenge for its earlier defeat, and then Oxford asserted its superiority again in the resumption of the series after an interval of seven years. Broughton refers to the casual state of the Club's organisation during his time, and struggles to remember if there was even a captain, which could not have helped preparations. As it was,

Taylor himself stepped into the bowling breach left by Kirwan's absence, taking four wickets in Oxford's first innings. However, he failed with the bat and it was left to extras with 55 to give Cambridge a useful lead. Cambridge's bowlers were even more profligate, allowing 63 extras second time around, and Cambridge was never likely to approach the target of 174, especially with two men mysteriously absent. Perhaps, given the waywardness of both sides' bowlers, there was after all a perfectly good reason why Kirwan stuck with underarm.

Taylor was captain by 1838, and he led by example, contributing scores of 65 and 73 to wins against the MCC and the Town. Kirwan was again absent from the Oxford match, and again his firepower was missed, despite Taylor's eleven wickets in the match. There were two further absentees, caused apparently by the death of George Seymour of King's College three days before the game. This was particularly strange, as neither of the players involved was from King's. Their loss probably made little difference to the result, a third successive walkover for Oxford. So began the continuous sequence of matches that has remained uninterrupted ever since, apart from the two World Wars.

1839 brought together the first great Cambridge team for the big match, including Kirwan for the first time, and the wicketkeeping skills of Thomas Anson. The fielding as a whole was first rate, and it offered excellent support to Kirwan, who showed what Cambridge had been missing by taking five wickets in Oxford's 50 innings of 88. Taylor finally came off in his last Varsity Match, notching Cambridge's first fifty in these encounters, and going on to 65 out of a total of 287. The rout was duly completed by an innings and 125 runs, Cambridge's first win against the old enemy, and the start of a wonderful sequence of five successive victories. As *Bell's Life* reported, the fixture at Lord's was beginning to fire the public's imagination. It attracted:

a numerous and fashionable assemblage of spectators. The splendid batting by the Cambridge gentlemen, we should think, completely wore out the bowlers, and many of the field. The fact was, the bowlers evidently at times lost their temper at not being enabled to disturb the wickets of their opponents.

In the first half of the 1840s, the Cambridge juggernaut was only stopped by rain in 1844, with Oxford beaten comfortably every other year apart from 1841. This game turned out to be something of a classic. Play was close and tense throughout, with scores being tied on first innings, and Oxford set an intriguing 121 to win. With seven wickets down, only 13 were needed, and Oxford seemed to be home. Garth hit a four for Oxford, but now Edward Sayres of Trinity bowled two of his colleagues for 0, leaving Lord William Ward, a future President of the MCC, to face the hat-trick ball. The fielding side never found out whether he would have survived, as his Lordship chose this precise moment to be inexplicably absent, and Cambridge had squeezed home by 8 runs in a cliffhanger. The real difference between the two sides appears to have been the fielding, especially that of the legendary long-stop Edward Hartopp, who saved countless byes off the faster bowlers.

FOUR

NEW HEADQUARTERS

At last, cricket was beginning to take hold, not only in the public imagination, but also among the student body. The local press began to sit up and take notice, and large crowds flocked to see the University play the MCC and the Town on Parker's Piece. But it was becoming increasingly clear that this 'village green' would not be suitable as a permanent home for the club now that the 'New' ground was defunct. Ford describes its character thus:

Its size was undeniable, and excellent were its wickets: but so large a sward, intersected by footpaths, public property with 'rights of way' innumerable, and no facilities for gate-money, was hardly the fit home for a University Club capable of measuring its strength with the strongest sides.

Even though the playing area had been levelled at the beginning of the 1830s, something more permanent needed to be found, away from the annoyances created by the mixing of townsfolk and students on the Piece.

As it turned out, the Club did not have long to wait for its new headquarters, provided by the entrepreneurial skills of Francis Fenner. Fenner had long been the scourge of the University, winning games for Cambridge Town almost single-handed with his hard hitting and fast bowling, notably in 1844 when he took no less than seventeen wickets in the match. By this time, he was not only a cigar merchant, but also a stockist of cricket equipment, including bats that gave 'a facility in vain looked for in any other'. By the mid-1850s, he had opened the 'University Gymnasium' at 6 Market Hill, and later ran a grocery before moving to the West Country in the 1860s. Of all his business interests, though, the ground that now bears his name is his lasting monument.

The first hint of a new development came on 4 April 1846, when the *Cambridge Independent Press* reported:

F. P. FENNER,
CIGAR MERCHANT,
RED HOUSE, PARKER'S PIECE, Cambridge.

BEGS respectfully to call attention of Cricketing Connoiseurs to his unequalled Stock of BATS which have been selected by himself with great care from the Repositories of the first makers. All that great experience could accomplish has been, in the adaptation of his Bats to the present improved style of playing; the wood being so scientifically placed, as to give an ease and elegance to the finished player, while to the mere tyro they afford a facility in vain looked for in any other.

BALLS, STUMPS, &c. Wholesale & Retail.

N.B.—None but Fenner's are used in the practice and great Matches of the University Club.[14 m

Fenner advertises his wares.

We understand the Earl of Stamford has engaged a field behind the Gaol for himself and friends, at a very handsome sum, as a private ground, where a quantity of men are engaged in preparing it under the superintendence of Lillywhite.

Frederick Lillywhite, in his *Guide to Cricketers*, confirms that the ground was first levelled by Lillywhite and Sons, contrary to the suggestion by Ford that it was Fenner that opened the ground in 1846. The ground, situated to the south of Parker's Piece, was already being used by the Earl in May 1846, in a match said to be between 'the Marylebone Club and eleven members of the University', although this game has not been officially recognised. It seems to have been an afterthought to the main game played the day before on Parker's Piece.

What appears to be the first mention by the press of Fenner's connection with the ground is on 1 April 1848, when the *Cambridge Chronicle* made this announcement:

A private ground situated at the back of the Town Gaol has been engaged by Mr Fenner, and during the whole winter men have been employed levelling and re-laying to the extent of 6½ acres. The ground is now completed, and promises to be one of the best private cricket grounds in the country. The University club have arranged to play all their matches there, and the advantages of a well-conducted private ground most people, we think, will be ready to appreciate.

Fenner's correspondence with the press later in the year makes it clear that he was approached by students with a view to procuring a ground, and that he decided he could make a ground of adequate size by adding another field to the one levelled by Lillywhite and already in use. He also refers to the refusal of the Town Club to move its games to his new ground, a decision seemingly based mainly on the fact that the general public would be charged admission, unlike on Parker's Piece.

A lithograph of the Town and University of Cambridge teams, published by Felix in 1847. Fenner is on the left of the middle group.

Immediately, the University Club became Fenner's tenants at a rent of £60 from May to September, and the ground officially opened to the public on 3 May with a single-wicket match, a variety of the game in which there is only one set of stumps, and only one batsman at a time. It was in vogue up to about 1850, being an excuse for gambling large sums of money on particular players. The game on this occasion was five-a-side, one team being led by the legendary John Wisden, while the other consisted of three undergraduates and two professionals. It proved to be a walkover for Wisden, who bowled all five of his opponents for 0, no doubt sending a lot of punters home happy.

The Club played its first match at Fenner's on 18 and 19 May, and, as the *Cambridge Chronicle* recorded, the improvement in facilities was immediately obvious:

Great satisfaction was expressed by all present at the comfort and additional pleasure available to all lovers of the game, many evident annoyances being removed… More than 500 spectators paid the small admission fee of 6d., and at different periods of the match the ground assumed a very interesting appearance.

On the field, the occasion was equally successful, the students beating the MCC by six wickets. Lent several men by the University, the MCC struggled in the face of Alfred Walker's underarm daisy-cutters, which were responsible for seven first-innings victims. Ultimately left 102 to win, the Club was guided home by the batting of Robert King, who was renowned more generally as a brilliant fielder at point. He made a crucial 46 not out, setting up a famous victory that augured well for the future of all concerned.

The excellent condition of the ground and the wicket at Fenner's has become a byword over the years, and indeed Fenner himself modestly claimed: 'Put a stump where you will and where you will, measure twenty-two yards, and you can play a game on any ground.' However, in the early years of the ground, the wicket itself left something to be desired, being made of long grass rather than rolled mud, and hence uneven. William Deacon, captain in 1850, backs this up:

I can certify that the ground was pretty rough, for I was knocked down senseless by a ball in the eye from 'young' Lillywhite.

The incident could have occurred in 1849, in the MCC match, as this was the only time that Deacon played against one of the famous Lillywhite clan for Cambridge. 'Young' Lillywhite would therefore be Frederick William, the patriarch of the family, who was already in his fifty-seventh year, but it is perhaps more likely that Deacon is referring to practising against one of Frederick's sons, John or James, both of whom were just starting out on their careers, and would have worked with their father in Cambridge. Contemporary newspapers are silent on the matter, but, whoever was the culprit, other incidents like this would have reached the ears of potential visitors. This perhaps explains the reluctance of Oxford to travel to Cambridge, and although Lord's was available the 1848 Varsity Match was once again played at the Magdalen ground.

It proved to be a remarkably even contest, with Oxford gaining only a 9-run first innings lead. Edward Blore, later president of the Club, and John Lee, who became Honorary Canon of Winchester Cathedral in 1877, bowled heroically to keep Cambridge well and truly in the hunt, but the target of 120 proved just too tough. In the last match of the season, against the Gentlemen of Kent, Lee proved his all-round worth by scoring Cambridge's first ever individual century, 110, in a good consolation win at Canterbury. The moment was particularly sweet, as it was the first time that Cambridge had beaten a side that could be said to represent a first-class county, containing as it did two of the greatest players of the time in Nicholas Felix and Alfred Mynn.

Blore continued in devastating form in 1849, as did King, who took over the captaincy from John Walker. His team went to Lord's as favourite, following two convincing wins against the MCC, and its confidence proved to be well founded. Blore took five wickets in each innings, and King was twice top-scorer, but it was his fielding and running between the wickets that made the real difference in a tight finish. The rumbustious nature of the game at the time is thrown into relief by an incident recalled by William Deacon:

I think it was in that match that King and the Oxford wicketkeeper, Joe Chitty, came into collision over a very short run. I can distinctly remember the momentary hush and then the roar of laughter, when it was seen that Chitty had lost his wig, and was sitting on the ground with the sun shining on his absolutely bald head. It was a very funny sight.

King managed to contain his mirth for long enough to see his side home, and went down from Cambridge safe in the knowledge that 'wig stopped play' was one of cricket's little foibles that was never likely to be repeated.

The 1850s were enlivened by several larger-than-life personalities, not the least of which was David Buchanan. He hailed from Edinburgh, and in his time at Cambridge, he developed into a fast left-arm bowler of some repute. After his seven wickets in the 1850 Varsity Match, Oxford must have been relieved the next year that he did not want to delay his trip back to Scotland after the end of term, and therefore missed the game at the beginning of July. Much later in life, he slowed his place right down, and had immense success, taking no less than eighty-eight wickets in Gentlemen *v.* Players matches, and 242 against the Universities, playing for teams like the Free Foresters.

Another great wandering club, I Zingari, first played Cambridge in 1851, a year that also saw the founding of the Quidnuncs. The name appears to have come from the phrase 'Quid nunc mortalia pectora cogit?', which translates roughly as 'What now calls our mortal breasts (more than cricket)?' Robert King was one of the three founding officers of this club, whose original aim was to provide holiday matches and games against the likes of Eton and Harrow. It soon developed into a way of providing a link between old and new Blues, and indeed a Blue became an automatic passport into the team. The club soon struck up a relationship with its Oxford counterpart, the Harlequins, but matches between the two seem to have ceased after about 1870. The Quidnuncs were finally revived in 1961, and there are now annual fixtures against the University, the Harlequins and the MCC. It maintains very vibrant links with the University Club, and can still attract quality players onto major tours, such as that of South Africa in 2002.

Meanwhile, back in the 1850s, Cambridge appointed Arthur Ward captain in 1854 in the hope that he might be able to halt Oxford's run of two consecutive innings victories. Ward became one of the club's most dedicated servants when his playing days were over, but he was not renowned for his batting ability or his athleticism. Weighing in at twenty stone, he was a complete liability in the field, much to the entertainment of spectators. The Lord's crowd was so merciless in its ribbing of him during the MCC match that year that he declined to play there against Oxford ten days later. Although *Bell's Life* states that Alfred Du Cane, a fresher from Harrow, took over for the match, Ward still tried to control events from the pavilion. However, he made matters considerably worse for himself by playing his opening bowler Joe McCormick as the wicketkeeper. In the end it was Cambridge's weak batting that led to a third successive drubbing by the old enemy with an innings to spare, leaving the series level at nine games each.

McCormick was one of the three treasurers who masterminded the building of the first pavilion at Fenner's in 1856, Robert Fitzgerald and Du Cane being the others. Fitzgerald became one of the MCC's most energetic secretaries in 1863, and also took an amateur team, including W.G. Grace, to North America in 1872. He was already wielding enough influence at Cambridge to start paying off the new building, which cost a total of £433 and five shillings. An elegant if basic facility,

The new pavilion compared with the accommodation on Parker's Piece, drawn in 1859 by J.L. Roget.

it was made of wood, and stood on the west side of the ground under the walls of the jail, a site now occupied by the university gymnasium. The fact that the debt had to be paid off in instalments indicated the perennially parlous state of the Club's finances, which were only augmented later in the century when the University Athletic Club began to share use of the ground.

Two more characters from the 1850s deserve our attention before we move on to the 'modern' era, ushered in by the legalisation of overarm bowling in 1864. Neither of them won much renown for their performances for Cambridge, but they both left an indelible mark in their own different ways. Indeed, Thomas Wills wasn't even at Cambridge. He was originally on the University's books, but never actually took up residence. However, when Cambridge was a man short for the 1856 Varsity Match, he stepped into the breach after Oxford raised no objection. He therefore has the unique distinction of obtaining his Blue without having matriculated, and he is also among the small band of players whose only game for Cambridge was in the Varsity Match. Our other hero, Henry Arkwright, managed four games for Cambridge in 1858, and was a good enough slow bowler to be regarded by David Buchanan as the inspiration for his switch to spin. His main hold on posterity, though, is through the tragic circumstances surrounding his early death. Buried by an avalanche on Mont Blanc in 1866, his perfectly preserved body was recovered from the glacier thirty-one years later, and finally laid to rest in the English cemetery at Chamounix.

A simmering controversy of these years was over the number of times a student could be allowed to obtain his Blue. Already three men had appeared five times for Oxford, a figure considered rather excessive, and Cambridge was determined to make an issue of it. When Cloudesley Marsham, Oxford captain in 1857, was reappointed for 1858, it was time to strike. Marsham would be up for his fifth Blue, and thus Cambridge came up with a proposal, recorded in the Club minute-book on 21 November 1857, to:

make an agreement in concert with the treasurers of the Oxford University Club to prevent any man of either University playing in the match between the two Universities, before he has resided at least one term, and after he has resided four academical years.

Such a rule would of course have excluded Wills from the reckoning, as well preventing Marsham and others from completing five years in the team.

Alas, Oxford was not entirely in concert with Cambridge on this, and waited until after the 1858 match to agree to a watered-down version that allowed a student to play five times for his University if he had to spend an extra year retaking his finals. This enabled Marsham to subject Cambridge to a humiliating innings defeat, including a personal second innings analysis of six for 17 as the Light Blues were routed for just 39, their lowest ever total against Oxford.

A final resolution of this knotty question had to wait until 1865, when Cambridge, incensed by the fifth appearance of R.D. Walker for Oxford, managed to persuade the Oxford committee to agree to the following rule:

That a man whose name is on the College books be qualified to play in the annual match between Oxford and Cambridge for the four consecutive years dating from the beginning of his first term of residence, and for those years only.

After all the fuss, this simple statement was enough to end any doubts over eligibility for many years. Only in the latter half of the twentieth century was the maximum raised to eight years, a figure not yet approached.

The intervening years had seen a temporary return to form by Cambridge, after a long fallow period. 1859 was an appalling season redeemed by a small win against Oxford, but the new decade dawned brightly. After another close win in a rain-sodden contest in 1860, the stage was set for a couple of dominant years, in which the University only lost once in eleven-a-side matches. That was to the Town in 1861, a defeat that was revenged amply in the return match. Cambridge won by an innings, and this turned out to be the last time the teams met.

One of the architects of this win was Henry Plowden, who became captain in 1862. He had considerable success with his off-breaks, and was highly regarded as a leader, but he was not the star of the team. That accolade was reserved for the Honourable Charles Lyttelton, son of Lord George Lyttelton, who had gained his Blue in 1838. Charles was later made Viscount Cobham, and had a son, also called Charles, who played against Oxford in 1908 and 1909. The family thereby became the first from Cambridge to be represented in the Varsity Match by three successive generations. Of Charles senior, Clement Booth, the 1864 captain, recalled:

he was without exception the best cricketer all round that I have ever played with;... a first-rate bat and a first-rate bowler, and he was also a very good wicketkeeper (though he wouldn't often go there if he could help it), and an excellent point and slip with an enormous arm-reach.

Aside from contributing seven wickets to a comfortable win in 1861, Lyttelton did not achieve much in the Varsity Match. His greatest triumph for Cambridge was a magnificent 128 in a win against the MCC in 1864, an innings characterised by his driving 'on the up', revolutionary for the time.

Performances had reached their peak with the fine side of 1862, whose victory against Oxford completed a quartet of successive wins. However, in 1863 another decline started, which was only arrested after four years. 1863 was notable for the official instigation of the 'Blue' in cricket, which had hitherto been the preserve of the rowers, who were in no hurry to share the privilege. Geoffrey Bolton, historian of the Oxford University Cricket Club, relates in his book how the impasse was solved:

… by a master-stroke of tact the President of the OUBC (luckily a passable cricketer) was elected to membership of the Harlequins, rightly a most exclusive club. The compliment was so much appreciated that all opposition was withdrawn and the Cricket Blue dates from 1863.

Thus, all cricket Blues prior to this date have only been awarded retrospectively.

The Varsity Match that year was a low-scoring affair, made infamous by the no-balling of Cambridge's Thomas Collins for throwing. It is still the only time this has occurred in the series, and indeed Collins was unlucky in the extreme. He was no-balled four or five times for having his bowling arm above the shoulder, and yet a year later this would have been legal, as overarm was finally allowed for the first time on 10 June, three days before the Varsity Match. Perhaps chastened by the experience, Collins never played first-class cricket again, confining his appearances to the Suffolk eleven.

Losing to Oxford in this period was no disgrace, as it was a superb outfit, especially in 1865. There was a definite turning of the corner in 1866, notably in the University's first victory against Surrey in a first-class match, described by *Bell's Life* as 'the best contested match of the season'. The Varsity Match was also exciting, culminating in a 12-run win for Oxford after Cambridge had controlled the first half of the game. Charles Absolom, a Trinity fresher, was a notable debutant in this game, and he made up for missing most of the summer by being the dominant personality in the side for the next two seasons, and indeed one of the greatest characters in the Club's history.

Absolom was known as the 'Cambridge navvy', presumably because of his penchant for haymaking and breakfasting on a quart of beer and a pint of gooseberries. Privately educated, he had no pedigree as a cricketer when he came up to Cambridge, and only slipped into the side after a recommendation from one of the Walker brothers, who had seen him play at Southgate. Ford refers to him in these terms:

He could play every stroke that was not in the books and very few that were to be found in them, but this may be due to the good-humoured malice of despairing bowlers, who found their best-length, straightest balls swept ruthlessly away to leg…

The hirsute Charles Absolom.

If his batting was unorthodox, his medium-paced bowling was from the textbook, and it brought him 101 wickets in eighteen matches for Cambridge. His fielding was brilliant, and his level of fitness was such that he was able to win the high jump for Cambridge in the University sports of 1867. He played a key role in beating Oxford in 1868, taking eight wickets and scoring 49 runs, and nearly pulled off a dramatic win against Surrey that year. Going like a train on 38, he managed to get hit by a throw to the wicketkeeper when scampering for a single. The umpire decided to give him out obstructing the field, much to the crowd's disbelief, and so Absolom secured his place in the record-books as the first man to be dismissed in this manner in first-class cricket.

'Charley' was given a further chance to be remembered by history when Lord Harris invited him to join his trip to Australia at the end of 1878. Along with three other Cambridge men, he made his debut in the only Test match of the tour at Melbourne. He made a typically whirlwind 52 in the first innings, helping to rescue England from the depths of despair, but he could not prevent a comprehensive defeat. There ended his Test career, but there is a tragic postscript to this story. Having blown all his money enjoying the Australian trip, Absolom was forced to make his living as a ship's purser, and in 1889 met a bizarre end when he was crushed by a falling cargo of sugar. Eccentric to the last, Absolom epitomised the spirit with which amateur sport was played in the Victorian era. Games were a 'manly' endeavour, but they were also entertainment, and Cambridge was never lacking in that with Absolom around.

FIVE

COMING OF AGE

The 1860s ended in fine style at Cambridge, beginning with the win against Oxford in 1868. Aside from Absolom's contribution, the key effort was that of the captain, Charles Green, who top-scored in each innings. Green came up from Uppingham in 1865 with a reputation as a fearsome fast bowler, but during his Cambridge days his batting skills took over, and he became, in Ford's words, 'a charming bat to watch, free and stylish to the last degree'. He scored 44 and 59 in an emphatic victory and, after Cambridge, went on to play a vital role in Essex's elevation to first-class status in 1894.

Green's departure at the end of the season merely made way for two even more colossal figures, both physically and metaphorically. Green's hitting powers were easily eclipsed by Charles Thornton, regarded by many as the hardest striker of a cricket ball ever to tread the earth. The veteran Cambridge journalist Percy Piggott, writing in 1948, described his style thus:

Thornton defied all modern ideas of protection by resolutely refusing to wear leg guards, and he would face the fastest bowlers with fearless equanimity. His reply to any question regarding leg protection was invariably the same: 'What is your bat for?' His batting was mainly of the 'death or glory' order; but he was always well satisfied if he could make a few lusty hits even though his stay was a short one.

This cavalier approach was not immediately apparent to his first Cambridge captain, Montagu Stow. Having averaged 41 in public school matches at Eton, Thornton was keen to keep up such a record, and played fairly cautiously in the early matches of 1869, reasoning, according to Stow, 'that a steady game was more certain to secure him a place' in the Varsity Match. This approach was soon abandoned, and by the time he went down to Lord's for the return match against the MCC, he was starting to unwind, scoring 33 and 34 in rapid time. Thornton peaked at the right time, scoring

Above left: *Charles Thornton, one of cricket's immortal hitters.*

Above right: *William Yardley, scorer of the first Varsity Match century.*

50 in only half an hour in the first innings against Oxford by playing his natural game. He followed this up with 36 in the second innings, made out of only 41 while he was in, getting off the mark with a massive on-drive that worried the inhabitants of the carriages on the boundary's edge. He had already hit a straight drive over the Lord's pavilion during the previous year's Eton *v.* Harrow match, and the greatest of his many stupendous hits over the years was a record 168 yards 2 feet made in the nets at Hove. The power of shot apparently came from big hips and loins, not from his forearms, which were small according to Ford. Incidentally, this was the first decade in which boundaries were used, and indeed the 1866 Eton *v.* Harrow match seems to have been the first instance at Lord's. This meant hits no longer had to be run out, but six was still not awarded unless, like Thornton's, the hit went right out of the ground.

Thornton was nicknamed 'Buns' by all and sundry, a legacy of his Eton days. As Lord Harris later explained, he was:

nicknamed 'Bun and Jam' at Eton – afterwards abbreviated to 'Buns' – because of an amusing incident… Thornton, in an interval when a wicket was down, bought a bun and jam, and commenced consuming it… A high catch was hit to him, which I fancy he caught. What happened to the bun I never heard for certain. Some say he swallowed it, others that he dropped it, others again that he crammed it, jam and all, into his trousers pocket.

Whatever happened to Thornton's snack, the modern reader will be relieved to know that at least the epithet does not refer to a particularly sensitive part of his anatomy.

If Thornton took a few games to get going for Cambridge, his fellow debutant William Yardley made an immediate impact by scoring 154 in the Freshman's trial match. This brought about his rapid elevation to the Varsity eleven, and he seized his chance with alacrity, top-scoring with 65 against the MCC and 34 out of 115 against the Gentlemen of England. The first game resulted in a convincing win for the students, but in the latter Yardley's innings was crucial in saving the match in the face of a continuous onslaught from Cambridge's old friend David Buchanan. Already he was attracting rave reviews for his style and skill, and was being mentioned in the same breath as W.G. Grace himself. There is no better description of Yardley at the wicket than that supplied by Ford:

A tall man, well over six feet, he played a most upright game, in every sense of the word, and being of powerful frame, put a great deal of force into his strokes. His driving and leg-hitting were perhaps his most brilliant hits, but his armoury was full of weapons. To the writer's mind he shares with W. Gunn and L.C.H. Palairet the reputation of being the most graceful of tall batsmen.

Throughout his life, Yardley grew accustomed to critical acclaim. He became a fashionable playwright in the 1870s, meeting with considerable success in comedies like *The Passport* and *Little Jack Sheppard*. As if that was not enough, his sporting prowess extended to a Blue in racquets, and he became a barrister of the Middle Temple in 1873. For the moment he was a member of a very strong Cambridge side that came into the Varsity Match unbeaten in first-class matches. After a 116-run win against the MCC spirits were high, and Cambridge batted consistently on another damp wicket. Absolom supported Thornton well with 30, and then helped Cambridge grab a crucial lead of 65, taking three top wickets, while the lob bowler Walter Money took six. Although the Light Blues could only muster 91 second time around, it was more than enough to secure a comfortable win thanks to Money's second six-wicket haul. The fielding of both sides had been exceptional, especially the wicket-keeping, Cambridge's Henry Richardson and Oxford's William Stewart managing to secure fourteen victims between them.

Although Absolom and Richardson had left, 1870 saw no discernible lessening of the team's powers. Money struck a particularly rich vein of form, top-scoring in the second innings of a victory against the MCC, followed by 85 in a winning draw against the Gentlemen, and a superb 134 in the eight-wicket defeat of Surrey. Yardley scored 90 not out in the second innings of that match, and Thornton also got his eye in with 65 against the Gentlemen, including a huge hit over the pavilion. Only a loss to the MCC in the return game cast a slight pall over proceedings, but the portents were certainly good for a fourth successive drubbing of the Dark Blues. As it turned out, it was the closest match in the history of this fixture, containing many fine individual performances, constant twists and turns, and a pulsating finish. But it has always been known as 'Cobden's Match', after Frank Cobden, an otherwise unexceptional fast bowler from Harrow and Trinity College. It was he who finished the game with a hat-trick, amid scenes of unbearable tension, to seal an unlikely win by 2 runs. Oxford came into the match slight favourites, although Cambridge had just completed a resounding victory against the MCC. Cambridge won the toss, and decided to bat despite the gloomy conditions that prevailed all day. There was a crowd of 8,000 on the first day, enjoying the social occasion as much as the play; 'Luncheons and flirtations were enjoyed with equal relish', said *Bell's Life*. Play commenced at 12.10 p.m., not at the advertised time of 11.30 a.m., a fact that Oxford lived to regret by the end of the game. Oxford's opening pair of Belcher and Francis bowled through most of the innings, and only A.T. Scott who, according to *The Times* 'played in a style that commended itself to every close observer' survived for very long, managing 45. A total of 147 was only just enough to keep Cambridge in the game. Oxford's reply was not much better, with Cobden and Ward warming up for their second innings exploits by taking seven wickets between them. Cobden, bowling fast and straight, had four victims, all of them clean bowled. The opener A.T. Fortescue was top scorer with 35. By the close of the first day, the innings was over, with Oxford in the lead by 28.

Frank Cobden, hero of the 1870 Varsity Match.

At the start of the second day, the crowd had swollen to 12,000, but it still had to wait until 11.55 a.m. for the beginning of Cambridge's second innings. The Light Blues fared no better this time around, losing five quick wickets for 40. The match seemed all but lost as William Yardley came to the wicket – Cambridge was only 12 runs ahead with five wickets left. In the face of continued hostile bowling from Francis, he and Dale put on 116 for the sixth wicket, and when Dale was finally out after two-and-a-half hours for a watchful 67, Yardley continued in the same vein, taking his score to 81 at lunchtime, when Cambridge had reached 176 for six. He reached his 100, the first ever in the Varsity match, soon after lunch, with a scampered single that nearly ran out Cobden at the other end. It took a brilliant piece of fielding to end his innings almost immediately afterwards. Francis induced a mishit drive, which he jumped high to knock up nearly twenty feet in the air, before catching it on its way down. Yardley had hit fourteen fours, batted about 110 minutes, and scored his runs out of 155 while he was at the wicket. It had been a 'most excellent innings, in which his fine and free hitting was only equalled by his strong and sturdy defence.'

The innings closed at 206, leaving Oxford 179 to win in a little under three hours. Francis had once again been their hero, bowling eighty-five four-ball overs in the match and finishing with twelve wickets. Oxford set off in pursuit at 4.10 p.m. The first wicket fell to Cobden for 0 in the third over, but Oxford nerves were steadied by a second-wicket stand of 72 between Fortescue and Ottaway. When 7 p.m., the official close of play, arrived, Oxford were poised for victory at 153-4, and 'as the game was considered lost to Cambridge, it was suggested by some that it would be well to finish it.' So the game continued after 7 p.m., but as the gloom of a London evening descended, Oxford subsided to 175 for seven, including the vital wicket of Ottaway after a three-hour vigil. Oxford was still favourite to win, needing only 4 more as Cobden took the ball at the Nursery End for his twenty-seventh over. Hill took a single off the first ball, which was to be the last he faced. Butler was then caught at mid-off – 176 for eight! Still, only 3 to win, but Belcher and Stewart were less than competent with the bat. There was a deathly hush in the crowd as Cobden sent down another fast, straight ball. Belcher could not lay a bat on it, and was bowled first ball – 176 for nine! R.H. Lyttelton, himself a member of a famous Cambridge clan, can now be left to describe what happened next:

Here then was the situation – Mr Stewart standing manfully up to the wicket, Mr Cobden beginning his run, and a perfectly dead silence in the crowd. Whiz went the ball; but alas! – as many other people… have done – the good advice is neglected, and Stewart, instead of following his captain's exhortations to keep his bat still and upright in the block-hole, just lifted it: fly went the bails, and Cambridge had won the match by 2 runs! The situation was bewildering. Nobody could quite realise what had happened for a second or so, but then – up went Mr Absolom's hat, down the pavilion steps with miraculous rapidity came the Rev A.R. Ward, and smash went Mr Charles Marsham's umbrella against the pavilion brickwork.

So, an incredible finish in circumstances reminiscent of many modern one-day games, and creating as much mayhem and confusion! Hill would live to regret giving up the strike off the first ball, and the Dark Blues must have wished that they did not live in such leisurely times, when the start of play on both days could be held up for no discernible reason. Surely they would have won if they had not lost more than an hour in this way. However that may be, just three balls had immortalised the name of Frank Cobden, whose hat-trick to finish the match is still unique in first-class cricket.

In the Club archive is a poignant set of correspondence that demonstrates only too well the fickle nature of fame, while shedding some light on the subsequent journey of the match ball. It begins with a letter dated 23 May 1908, on the letterhead of Cobden's Hotel, Capel Curig, North Wales. In the letter, Cobden says that, on the advice of Lord Harris, he has decided to enquire how much the Club might be prepared to offer for the ball. He goes on to explain that he would have been very happy to donate the ball for free, but 'everything is gone wrong with me and I am next door to a pauper'. In a later letter, he mentions the agreed price of £10, and points out that this cancels out what he paid for the ball:

It cost me £10 to get hold of it, for when the last wicket fell Yardley got hold, and as I had lent him £10 a few days before he said he would stick to it unless I let him off… the tenner, and in the excitement I agreed.

The last letter is dated 1 August, and leaves an address in Salisbury, which, he says, 'will always find me'. It seems then that his hotel was, at least temporarily, struggling, but Cobden died at Capel Curig in 1932, his fortunes sufficiently revived to keep him to a healthy old age. 'Cobden's match' was definitely the highlight of his career, but there were other crucial contributions that made it all possible. In addition to Yardley's groundbreaking hundred, the batting of John Dale and Edward Ward's bowling must not be forgotten. Dale was a product of Tonbridge school and only its fourth Cambridge cricket Blue. Renowned for being stylish but fairly defensive, he was the perfect foil for Yardley, and could have reached a hundred as well if Ottaway had not dismissed him with a brilliant catch on the boundary. He later contributed to the tension in Oxford's innings by dropping a vital catch when his attention was diverted by a young lady in the crowd. Ward's second-innings spell was perhaps the biggest factor of all in deciding the fate of the match. He bowled thiry-two four-ball overs of fast left-handed round-arm, taking six for 29 in a superbly sustained spell, but, like Cobden, there were to be no further peaks in his career.

Yardley was rewarded for his mature approach with the captaincy for 1871, but his team could not keep up its run of form. After a sound defeat at the hands of the MCC, Cambridge played host to the twenty-two-year-old W.G. Grace for the first time. Representing the Gentlemen of England, he made an immediate and lasting impression by scoring 162, including a century before lunch on the first day. Cambridge never recovered from the shock, and although Thornton hit 20 off a Buchanan over on his way to a spectacular 74, Grace finished the students off with seven wickets in the second innings. The Gentlemen were not required to bat again. The only first-class win of the season was at The Oval against an ailing Surrey side that was languishing near the bottom of the unofficial championship. Frederick Fryer, naturally enough known as 'Tuck', steered Cambridge home in another thrilling finish, hitting the winning runs at 7.30 p.m. on the last evening. Fryer was another stylish batsman from Harrow who performed consistently for Cambridge, but never did himself justice against Oxford. At least he had helped make the trip to Lord's a more pleasurable one, but any high spirits were soon dampened by a miserably wet return match against the MCC, the last warm-up before the Varsity Match. Cambridge's bowling was not strong enough to exploit the conditions fully, and the second innings finished with a disastrous total of 45; hardly ideal preparation for the big day.

Oxford, in contrast, had managed a convincing performance in the corresponding fixture, also marred by rain. Although the match was drawn, Oxford was clearly on top at the close, thanks to the inspired fast bowling of Samuel Butler, who took eight for 25. The formbook was proved correct in dramatic fashion when Butler faced the Light Blues on the same turf. Oxford made a respectable 170 on a treacherous wicket, but when Cambridge batted it appeared to be a totally different game. Money made 23 and Yardley 25, but from 62 for four, the last six wickets fell for only 3, and Cambridge was forced to follow on. The sole architect of the collapse had been Butler, who had taken all ten wickets for only 38, and had been unstoppable with his unrelenting mixture of shooters and bumpers. The second innings saw greater resolution from the batsmen, but Butler took five more, and Oxford had an easy task knocking off a handful of runs. If 'Cobden's match' had been something of a misnomer, there was no disputing that 1871 was truly 'Butler's year', for never was there a clearer example of one man making the difference between two sides.

Yardley helped to exact a crushing revenge a year later, and in doing so made himself significantly wealthier. On the day of the 1870 win he had been offered 10–1 that another century would not be scored in the Varsity Match for the next ten years, odds he accepted with alacrity. His 130 out of Cambridge's 388 (both records at the time) contained twenty fours and occupied no more than 125 minutes. In the face of such a large total, the demoralised Dark Blues crashed to defeat by an innings and 166 runs, a margin of victory that remained a Varsity Match record for fifty-one years. The bowling honours were taken by Walter Powys, a fast bowler from Pembroke College, who bagged thirteen victims in the match. It was thought that the result of the 1873 match, a three-wicket win to Oxford, would have been different if Powys had been available, but, sadly, he was out of the country that year.

Events on the pitch were rather overshadowed by the internal affairs of the Club, in particular the appointment of the Reverend Arthur Ward as president under Article 3 of the Revised Laws, which stated:

That the President be elected by the Club from the Lessees of the Ground, and that this appointment be, as far as possible, a permanent one.

An advertisement for the sale of the contents of the original pavilion.

The significance of the appointment was not lost on Ward, who used his new powers to tackle an issue that had already been identified as urgent in 1871:

The Pavilion on Fenner's Ground has fallen into such a state of dilapidation that to repair it would cost a considerable sum of money… the Pavilion is altogether too small to accommodate the great numbers who now use the ground.

The total cost of building a new pavilion was then estimated at £900, but it seemed that the uncertainty of the Club's tenure of the ground prevented subscribers coming forward. Ward, in typically forthright fashion, secured the ground for thirty-five years, and invited tenders for the new pavilion. After the architect, W.M. Fawcett, had initially estimated £1,500 for the project, on 24 March 1874 a tender of £1,987 was accepted from a Mr Loveday. In time-honoured fashion, the costs escalated month by month, until, by the time of its opening in the summer of 1875, the total bill was nearly £4,000. As a piece of grand architecture, the new building met with immediate approval. A contemporary press report describes the interior in glowing terms:

The woodwork is beautifully carved and interlaced with the emblems of cricket. The chimney piece is of stone, richly moulded from the quarries of Bromsgrove, Worcestershire… design, not patchwork; and a solidity that will long bear the strain of the elastic step and the silent gnawings of the common enemy – Time.

At last the Club had a pavilion fit for classical scholars and athletes. Would it assist the team's performance on the pitch? It could certainly do no harm and neither, it seemed, could a lavish dinner held in Ward's honour on 4 June. Fortified by 'Filets de Pigeons á la Dauphine' and 'Crevettes sur Glacé', the students completed a fine win against the Gentlemen of England the next morning.

The 1875 side was greatly strengthened by the inclusion of two immensely gifted Freshmen in Alfred Lucas and the Honourable Edward Lyttelton. Lucas added style and ballast to the batting, although he did not score heavily in his first season. Like Absolom, he played for England on Lord Harris' tour, and continued his career into the early years of the twentieth century. Lyttelton, son of the fourth Lord, who had represented Cambridge in the 1830s, was briefly one of the best amateur batsmen in England, but gave up the game to devote himself to teaching, later becoming headmaster of both Haileybury and Eton. The year was further made memorable by the incredible wicket-taking feats of the slow round-arm bowler, Charles Sharpe. He set up a new Cambridge season's record by taking sixty-six wickets in only seven games, including eleven in the Varsity Match. The latter feat was to no avail, however, as in another incredibly tense finish Oxford won by just 6 runs to take a one-match lead in the series. Like so many of his ilk, Sharpe became a man of the cloth, and faded into obscurity after just one season.

The menu for the dinner in honour of A.R. Ward in 1875.

The second half of the 1870s saw the gradual emergence of perhaps the most powerful all-round squad assembled in the long history of the Club, but initially it was the batting that impressed with its depth. Lucas began 1876 with a 100 and a 50 against C.I. Thornton's XI, and Lyttelton's brother Alfred started his Cambridge career with an impressive 78 in the same match. With only a defeat by the Gentlemen of England to blot its copybook, Cambridge approached Lord's as clear favourite to draw level in the Varsity series. It duly did so with consummate ease, winning by nine wickets with most of the last day to spare. It owed most to William Patterson, educated like Lucas at Uppingham, who hit a not-out century coming in at number seven and took seven wickets in all. Alfred Lyttelton ran himself out with the scores level, seemingly after a wager with Lucas over who would make the winning hit. Lucas duly hit the next ball first bounce into the pavilion.

This story illustrates the more extrovert nature of Alfred as compared with Edward, and it carried through into all aspects of their lives. As a batsman, Edward was a stylist while Alfred relied on power. As a rather tall wicketkeeper, Alfred did not regard himself as a quick stumper, but was a brilliant catcher. Both were outstanding in other ball sports, Alfred excelling at racquets and tennis, while Edward gained his Blue for the less glamorous sport of fives. Typically, when it came to football, Alfred was a fast and powerful forward, although 'a little deficient in ball control', but Edward preferred to languish back in defence. He described his brother's forward style in heroic terms:

When things grew to be exciting his ardour waxed to a formidable heat, and he would come thundering down with the heavy knees far advanced and all the paraphernalia of a Homeric onset.

Both played for the Old Etonians in the FA Cup final of 1876, although they lost 3-0 to Wanderers in the replay. They also both obtained a single international cap against Scotland. But it was in his chosen career as a politician that Alfred saw most of the limelight, being an MP for the last eighteen years of his life, and rising to the heights of Secretary of State for the Colonies in 1902.

1877 was a year of mixed fortunes on the pitch, two convincing wins against Surrey failing to make up for a disappointingly heavy loss in the Varsity Match. Some consolation was offered the day after the game by a dinner to mark the Golden Jubilee of the fixture. It was held at the Cannon Street Hotel, and numbered 120 old players among the guests, including six from the very first game. Sir Herbert Jenner-Fust, as he now was, made an entertaining speech full of reminiscences, and the Reverend C.S. Bere of the 1851 Oxford eleven composed a special song for the occasion. It begins thus:

Fifty years have sped since first,
Keen to win their laurel,
Oxford, round a Wordsworth clustered,
Cambridge under Jenner mustered,
Met in friendly quarrel.

A veil may safely be drawn over the remaining verses, but it was sung on the night, and seems to have hit the required spot. The Light Blues were further heartened by a one-off donation of £100 from the MCC, although it still refused to share the profits from the match with either side.

Cambridge had a good side, but not yet a great one. There was still a piece missing from the jigsaw, and it was Allan Steel who supplied it. After only two games, *Bell's Life* was admiring the 'powerful array of talent' at Cambridge's disposal, and there was no doubt who was the centre of that power. Steel had been a brilliant schoolboy cricketer at Marlborough, and had already made his debut for Lancashire when he enrolled at Trinity Hall. He bowled slow leg-breaks, interspersed with occasional off-breaks, and as a batsman had a full range of strokes that he unfurled frequently throughout his career. He caused a sensation at Cambridge with thirty-one wickets in his first three games, and he never let up throughout the season. In eight games, he took seventy-five wickets at an astonishing average of 7.42, and also topped the batting averages with 339 runs at 37. It was not a high-scoring year but, although Cambridge didn't top 300 all season, it completed a superb run with wins against Oxford and Australia at Lord's. The record of eight wins in eight games remains the only 100 per cent record Cambridge has ever had, and Steel had made it all possible.

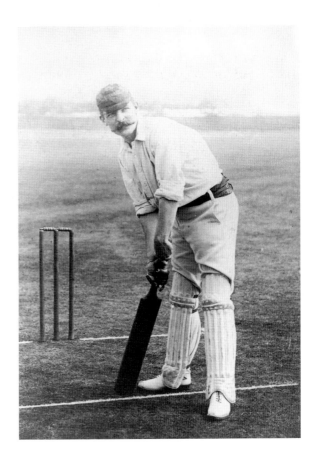

A.G. Steel, Cambridge's greatest all-rounder.

Yet Cambridge was by no means a one-man band. Under the stewardship of Alfred Lyttelton in 1879, several names came to the fore and ensured another unbeaten record. The Honourable Ivo Bligh, another tall, powerful batsman, came second in the averages behind Lyttelton, and produced the performance of the season with a brilliant 113 not out against Surrey. He is now known principally as the captain on the 'Ashes' tour of 1882/83, but he was a fine player in his own right until ill health forced his retirement. The attack was bolstered by Philip Morton, a fast bowler from Rossall, and Hugh Wood, a slow left-armer from Sheffield. Between them they snared sixty-nine victims in the six games played, and proved an admirable foil for Steel. When it came to the Varsity Match, though, Steel again reigned supreme. He finished Oxford's first innings by taking a hat-trick, the last two clean bowled, and then proceeded to top score in Cambridge's reply. His 64 helped the Light Blues to a significant lead of 49, and, after Oxford's worst score of 32 the previous year, it would not have been surprising if Cambridge had won by an innings. As it was, Steel's seven for 23 left Cambridge with only 16 to make, and this time Lyttelton did score the winning runs just before a torrential downpour.

The Hon. Ivo Bligh, as depicted by 'Spy'.

SIX

FROM THE STUDDS TO SAMMY

To have one top quality all-rounder in the side was a blessing, but to have two was little short of miraculous. In 1880, Steel was joined by Charles Studd, brother of George, who had made his entrance the year before. Their father Edward, a man of leisure who enjoyed a flutter, had been converted to Christianity by seeing the American evangelists Moody and Sankey, and Charles was destined to follow in his footsteps despite initial scepticism. At Eton, he set up a Bible class, and continued to proselytise in a quiet way at Cambridge. After his student days, the call of the Lord became overpowering, and in 1884 he joined the China Inland Mission with Samuel Smith, a rowing Blue, and five other Cambridge graduates, who collectively became known, naturally enough, as the 'Cambridge Seven'. After a life of many privations, his lasting legacy in terms of Christian history was to found the Heart of Africa Mission in the Belgian Congo, where he died in 1931. In the pantheon of cricket, Charles Studd is perhaps best remembered for being the non-striker who watched helplessly as the last English wicket fell in the dramatic 'Ashes' defeat at The Oval in 1882. However, in his brief career, he established nearly as great a reputation as Steel for his all-round play. Described by Ford as 'a powerful commanding batsman and a slow bowler who seldom sent up a bad ball', he topped the national batting averages in 1882 and, in thirty-one games for Cambridge, scored 1,852 runs at an average of 39.4, and took 130 wickets at 16.3. His brothers George and Kynaston, the eldest, were also useful if less-talented batsmen, and together they formed a triumvirate known as the 'shirtfront', a nickname that had rather more resonance in those days of greater sartorial elegance. Between them, they had a great deal to do with the success of the team in the early 1880s, and in 1882 they became the first trio of brothers to play in the Varsity Match, a feat not repeated until 1921, when the Ashton brothers played for Cambridge.

In Charles Studd's second match, Cambridge notched a notable success against Yorkshire, in no small part due to the batting of Bligh and Studd, who scored 68,

Above left: *C. T. Studd in Africa, two years before his death.*

Above right: *The Studd brothers in their Cambridge days.*

and the bowling of Steel, who took eleven wickets. The second half of the season belonged to Steel, who put on an awesome all-round display. He scored a 50 and took five wickets against the Gentlemen of England, a twelve-a-side game in which the University notched a new highest score of 593, and then a brilliant 118 and eight wickets in yet another defeat of Surrey. In the traditional pre-Varsity encounter with the MCC, he top-scored in each innings and took a further ten wickets, but it was not enough to prevent defeat by 49 runs. Against Oxford he had another ten-wicket haul, but he was upstaged in the first innings by Morton who, like Steel the previous year, took a hat-trick. Unlike Steel, he needed no assistance from the fielders, bowling Fowler and Harrison, and having Evelyn leg before wicket. A spirited stand of 51 for the last wicket prevented the follow-on, but Charles Studd's 52 ensured a target well beyond Oxford's grasp, and Cambridge swept home for the third time in a row.

1881 saw a settled side under Ivo Bligh's captaincy. Once again the Gentlemen of England's attack was put to the sword, with all eleven of the opposition turning their arms over, but once again time ran out with Cambridge in a winning position. The coup of the season came in the next game, when the students inflicted on Lancashire its only defeat of the season. George Studd played a magnificent lone hand, carrying his bat for 106 out of 187, made in 190 minutes with fourteen fours. What made the innings even more special was the fact that Charles and Kynaston had both scored hundreds in the previous innings against the Gentlemen. George's brilliance was rewarded with a famous seven-wicket win, thanks to Steel's eleven wickets against his home county in the first match played on the new Liverpool ground. The season was a triumph for George and Charles Studd, as they both scored over 500 runs, but ultimately it was a failure for Cambridge when it stumbled at the final hurdle. Its bowling resources were not quite what they had been, whereas Oxford had the unpredictable fast bowling of Alfred Evans. His thirteen wickets were decisive in the Dark Blues' comfortable win, and forced Cambridge to look harder for new blood that could add greater penetration to the attack.

The answer soon came in the shape of Charles Aubrey Smith, a fast bowler from Charterhouse, who impressed all observers with his eight for 60 in the Freshmen's match at the start of 1882. His cricketing talent was already apparent, but there had so far been few signs of the acting ability that led to a successful Hollywood career, although he did join an amateur dramatic group called the 'Thespids' on coming up to Cambridge. He made an immediate impact for the Light Blues, taking five for 17 on debut, and helping dismiss an MCC twelve for a feeble 46. It was in the next match, against C.I. Thornton's XI, that he gained his nickname of 'round the corner', after Thornton himself had used the phrase to describe a run-up that began at mid-off. He had been assisted in the defeat of the MCC by another bowler with

C. Aubrey Smith in Hollywood.
Boris Karloff is the wicketkeeper.

an unusual action, Robert Ramsay. Known as 'Twisting Tommy' because of his corkscrew action. Ramsay was born in Cheltenham, but brought up on a sheep farm in Queensland, before returning to England to complete his education. His leg-breaks were to bring him fifty-eight victims in the season, including thirteen in that first match.

Another win against Lancashire was a perfect warm-up for the visit of the mighty Australians, who came to Cambridge at the end of a ten-week-long unbeaten sequence. The crowds flocked to Fenner's at the prospect of seeing Spofforth and co., and the sun shone brightly in anticipation. Murdoch won the toss and batted on a belter of a pitch, but the tourists could make nothing of the contrasting bowling of Ramsay and Charles Studd, who took five wickets apiece as the Australians crumbled. Three wickets were down for 55 in Cambridge's reply when Charles Studd joined his brother George:

At 89 Spofforth clean bowled G.B. for a brilliant but somewhat lucky innings of 42. Bather now became C.T.'s partner and a most determined resistance was offered to the Australian bowling... up to the call of time, C.T.... was not out 85... he thoroughly deserved the enthusiastic reception that greeted him... playing against bowling that was quite new to him, he never seemed at a loss to know what to do with it, and was never in any way nervous.

Cambridge gained a first-innings lead of 127, thanks to a superb 118 by Studd, and 26 byes, let through by Billy Murdoch, a stopgap wicketkeeper in the absence of the legendary Blackham. Although the visitors made a much better fist of things second time around, Ramsay's seven wickets meant the target was always going to be within reach. This time, George and Kynaston Studd posted the first century partnership made against Australia on this trip, and the students cruised to a memorable six-wicket win. With this momentum behind them, the Varsity Match was almost a formality, and indeed it followed almost exactly the same pattern as the Australian game, except this time George Studd made the hundred, and the victory margin was seven wickets.

1882 had seen the debut of two more great names in Cambridge cricket, the Honourable Martin Bladen Hawke, and Charles Wright. Both showed themselves at their best in 1883, and both made a lasting impact on the game after their student days. Hawke was a descendant of the Admiral Hawke who had fought the French at the battle of Quiberon Bay, and became the seventh Baron Hawke in 1887. He took to the Yorkshire captaincy as to the manner born, and stayed in the job until 1911, seeing the county through one of its most successful periods. He was renowned for ensuring that the professionals under his charge were looked after, provided they behaved themselves. Never afraid to court controversy, his most famous gaffe was: 'Pray God, no professional shall ever captain England.' While many might secretly have agreed, very few were game to put their heads above the parapet and say so. In his autobiography, he professed similarly reactionary views concerning candidates for the Cambridge elevens against Oxford:

Given nearly similar cricketing powers, there is not the slightest doubt that an Etonian or Harrovian should have the greatest chance, because he has already had his baptême de feu *in facing a big crowd at Lord's.*

Needless to say, Lord Hawke was educated at Eton.

'Chawles' Wright, as he was known to his contemporaries, may have been rather taken aback by such sentiments, having been to Charterhouse himself, and playing in an era where the old domination of the top schools was finally being challenged. Wright was another player off Cambridge's production line of wicketkeeper–batsman, although after Cambridge his stumping skills declined. He was a man for the big occasion, averaging 49 in the Varsity Match, and showed admirable patience as an opening batsman. His Achilles' heel was his lethargic running between the wickets, which prompted Hawke to recount that, once, on being called for a short run, he exclaimed: 'Do you take me for a blooming archangel that you think I can fly?' As a wicketkeeper, he was involved in one record that must have haunted him for some time. Against Yorkshire in 1884, he shared the gloves with Cecil Knatchbull-Hugessen, an occasional wicketkeeper. Regrettably, between them they let through 57 byes, a world record that very few have attempted to outdo in the intervening years.

Before that, however, both Wright and Hawke were to be involved in another triumphant year, under the captaincy of Charles Studd. Studd himself led by example, topping both batting and bowling averages, and beating Surrey almost single-handed with a magnificent 175 not out. The only loss was in the first match of the season

C. T. Studd's magnificent 175 not out helped defeat Surrey in 1883.

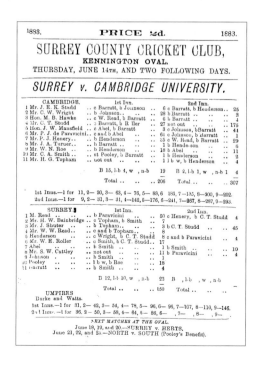

against the MCC, but after that the last seven games brought five wins and two draws. According to *Wisden*, 'some of the finest batting of the season' was contained in a stand of 160 between the captain and Hawke against C.I. Thornton's XI. Hawke made 141, his only century for Cambridge, and showed that he was a good enough batsman to merit a place, even without his aristocratic connections. And so to Lord's, where the Light Blues once again found themselves favourites. They owed much to Wright's application, which brought him a century in three-and-a-quarter hours, and helped raise a respectable 215 in damp conditions. The luck was all on Cambridge's side, as Oxford was caught on a drying wicket on the second morning, losing all ten wickets for 28 as it slumped to 55 all out. Although Oxford matched Cambridge's total in the follow-on, Wright made sure he was still there at the finish on 29 not out, guiding his side to another comfortable seven-wicket win.

Kynaston Studd took over the captaincy in 1884, completing a sequence of three years in a row in which the Studd brothers had been at the helm. Unfortunately, as *Wisden* summed it up in typically pithy fashion, it was 'a most disastrous season'. The loss of Charles Studd vitally affected both batting and bowling. The sole victory was against the Gentlemen, as against seven defeats, and the depths to which Cambridge's batting sank are shown by the fact that seven hundreds were scored against the students, while they could not manage one between them. The only note of cheer during the season came during the Gentlemen's visit to Cambridge, when two of their number penned an ode to Arthur Ward, still president of Cambridge, and renowned for his lavish hospitality towards visiting amateurs. Here is a flavour of the tribute:

C. U. C. C.

MATCHES FOR 1884.

At the "University" Ground.

May 7, 8	.........TWO ELEVENS OF SENIORS.
,, 9, 10	.........TWO ELEVENS OF FRESHMEN.
,, 15, 16, 17	...ELEVEN *v.* SIXTEEN.
,, 22, 23, 24	...UNIVERSITY *v.* ENGLAND.
,, 26, 27, 28	...UNIVERSITY *v.* YORKSHIRE.
June 2, 3, 4	......UNIVERSITY *v.* GENTLEMEN OF ENGLAND.
,, 9, 10, 11	...UNIVERSITY *v.* M.C.C. & GROUND.
,, 16, 17, 18	...UNIVERSITY *v.* AUSTRALIANS.

Play commences at 12.
Interval for Lunch 2—2.45.
Stumps drawn at 6.30.

At the "Oval."

June 19, 20, 21 ...UNIVERSITY *v.* SURREY.

At "Lords."

June 23, 24, 25 ...UNIVERSITY *v.* M.C.C. & GROUND.
June 30, July 1, 2..OXFORD *v.* CAMBRIDGE.

ARTHUR R. WARD, *President & Treasurer.*
J. E. K. STUDD, *Captain.*
M. B. HAWKE, *Secretary.*
C. W. WRIGHT, *Assistant Treasurer.*

Member's Signature ....

Members omitting to produce their Tickets on Match days will be charged the usual Admission Fee, which will be refunded on application to the Treasurer.

The fixture list for 1884.

Oh Bollinger! Oh Bollinger!
A bumper toast we drain
To thee, thy eggs, thy sausages,
Thy salmon, thy champagne.

Oh Bollinger! Oh Bollinger!
Well known on Fenner's sward,
Whatever would we do without
Your jests, O Mr Ward?

In addition to entertaining, Ward was well known for his little foibles, such as his ban on walking-sticks and dogs in the pavilion. The story goes that the Reverend James Porter, Master of Peterhouse and treasurer of the Club, got round the rule by paying for his dog Hugo to be a life member, a gesture that even Ward had to see the funny side of.

The decline continued in 1885, despite Hawke's imperious captaincy. Coming into the Varsity Match, Cambridge had not won a single game, but neither had Oxford, and Cambridge had at least had the better of two of its drawn games. As it happened, the match was swung in the Light Blues' favour by a remarkable opening stand of 152 between Wright and Herbert Bainbridge, a match record at that time. Bainbridge was yet another stylish product of Eton and Trinity, good enough for Hawke to consider him close to an England call if not for his slowness in the field. After such a bright opening, the rest of the batting was disappointing, but a lead of 151 on first innings was always going to be enough. Aubrey Smith picked up another five wickets, all clean bowled, leaving a modest target of 89 for victory. Freakishly, Cambridge's winning margin was yet again seven wickets, the fourth year in a row that this had occurred. After fifty-one games, Cambridge had won twenty-six, Oxford twenty-three, and there had been two draws. For the first time there was daylight between the two teams, and ever since Cambridge has nurtured it, turning a chink into a positive shaft that Oxford has never been able to obliterate.

Bainbridge took over the captaincy in 1886, and he could not have set a good example as an athlete, for *Wisden* commented unfavourably on Cambridge's fielding twice in successive years, calling it 'slovenly' in 1886 and 'unworthy of a University team' in 1887. If the fielding was poor, general playing standards were picking up again, leading to a record of five wins and three losses in nine games. The season started with an impressive sequence of three wins, all of them after being behind on first innings. Indeed, two of them were completed after the students had been forced to follow on. On the first occasion, against C.I. Thornton's XI, the fightback was led by John Turner from Uppingham, a batsman of the 'slashing type' according to Ford. Ironically, he was regarded as one of Cambridge's finest ever fielders, with a prehensile reach and a rifling return to the wicketkeeper. In this match, he played the innings of his life, an epic 174 made in four hours against an attack that included the ferociously fast Jack Crossland. The second match was against Yorkshire, and this

Frank Marchant, a popular captain in 1887.

time the man who helped wipe off a first-innings deficit of 80 was George Kemp. After becoming an MP at the age of twenty-nine, Kemp was made Baron Rochdale in 1913 for services to his constituency. For the moment, he was waging his own private War of the Roses, scoring centuries both in this game and in the return match at Sheffield, although Yorkshire won the latter by seven wickets.

The man who stamped his name on this season, though, was Claude Rock, the son of a Tasmanian doctor. He had first come to prominence in the 1884 Varsity Match, when, in a vain attempt to save the game, he lived up to his name by scoring 56 in three hours and twenty minutes. While his batting was never attractive, his bowling won enough plaudits for him to be recognised by *Lillywhite's Annual* as the best bowler at an English university. Bainbridge went further:

He was slow-medium in pace, and had a long arm that came over with a majestic swing like a fly-wheel. He broke back just the right amount, and spun the ball well. In 1886 no one really collared him, and… he was probably the best amateur slow bowler of the day.

Certainly, as far as the figures go, there is not much argument with his captain's assessment, as Rock took sixty-five wickets in eight games at a healthy average of 13.35. He had eight five-wicket hauls, including a best of seven for 37 in the defeat of the MCC at Lord's. His teammates must have felt confident that Rock would give them the edge against the old enemy, and he didn't disappoint, taking five wickets in each innings. Unfortunately, the batsmen, apart from Bainbridge, let him down badly. Even so, there would have been little in it, if there had not been

The Tasmanian-born all-rounder Claude Rock.

a remarkable passage of play at the start of Oxford's second innings. The openers, Kingsmill Key and William Rashleigh, put on 243 for the first wicket, a record for the match that still stands. The scorecard looks remarkably lopsided, as every other batsman was dismissed in single figures, but they had done more than enough to bury Cambridge's challenge for another year.

About the 1887 season, the less said the better. Although runs were never a problem, the bowling was too weak to provide adequate back-up; Cambridge scored 534 in a drawn game against Sussex, only to be trounced by an innings in the next match by Surrey, who scored 543. A win against C.I. Thornton's XI in the first match was the only success of the season, and Oxford again completed an easy victory at Lord's. A curiosity of this match was the fact that the last men to be selected for both sides, Eustace Crawley of Cambridge and Lord George Scott of Oxford, both scored hundreds. Crawley never really came off again, but he did achieve further fame in the field of combat, being Mentioned in Dispatches during the Boer War, before dying in action on the battlefields of Belgium in 1914. Meanwhile, Cambridge was in need of heroes of its own, and sure enough the next summer produced two such cricketers whose student careers were so inextricably linked that they could have been twins.

The elder of the 'twins' was Sammy Woods, a fine physical specimen from Glenfield, near Sydney, who trained on the way to school by sparring with deckhands on the Manly ferry. Sent to England to finish his education, he became a leading personality at Brighton College where, in addition to rugby and cricket, he spent his time playing football and billiards, and going beagling and fox-hunting. One of his many legendary schoolboy feats was taking fourteen for 27 in a match against

Sammy Woods.

Lancing College, all of them clean bowled. Not renowned for his scholastic abilities, as soon as he arrived at Jesus College he joined two august clubs, the Rhadegund (devoted to port wine) and the Natives (for aficionados of the oyster). Needless to say, he was later elected president of both. But Sammy also needed more physical outlets for his extrovert personality, and he found them on the rugby field in the winter and at Fenner's in the summer. When spring finally arrived in 1888, Sammy got straight into the swing of things by scoring 98 in the Freshmen's match, but after that it was not his use of the long handle that stood out, but his fast bowling. Not only was he extremely fast in his undergraduate days, but he was also accurate and able to bowl for long spells without tiring. Contrary to his academic reputation, he was regarded by Sir Pelham Warner as the most intelligent of fast bowlers, able at will to mix up searing yorkers with cunningly disguised slower balls. While he was around, Cambridge held a clear advantage over Oxford, but he couldn't do it all on his own – like all great bowlers, he needed a partner in crime.

The man who filled that role was a dour Scotsman, the polar opposite to Woods in terms of temperament, but they obviously got on well enough to share rooms overlooking Jesus Common for their last two years in residence. Like Woods, Gregor MacGregor was an international rugby player, and indeed they played against each other in the England *v.* Scotland clash of 1891. Also like Woods, he played cricket for England, but never when his old Cambridge chum (who also played for Australia) was in the opposition. Often the victim of his friend's high-spirited japes, Sammy went too far on the eve of a Varsity Match. He managed to knock MacGregor

Gregor MacGregor.

against a plate-glass window, through which he duly fell. It is not clear from the available accounts whether he cut his hands or not, but he still kept wicket the next day. A contrite Woods called it the worst day of his life. Although a useful lower-order batsman, this story emphasises that MacGregor was most of all a consummate and brave wicketkeeper, the only one who would stand close to the wicket to Sammy's thunderbolts. MacGregor's contemporary Digby Jephson paid tribute to their symbiotic relationship as follows:

The faster Sam bowled, the nearer the sticks stood Mac, and he took the five-and-a-half ounces of leather, cork and string, as if it were a ping-pong ball! He took it on the off or the on-side with equal facility, and he would throw the ball back, time in and time out, with the suggestion that he was a little tired of the simplicity of it all.

With such a brilliant pair working in tandem, the rest of the team was naturally lifted to a level that *Wisden* declared was 'decidedly above the average' in 1888, with even better prospects to come.

It was a hideously wet summer, which prevented a positive result in three of the nine games. Of those three, the performance against the Australians was perhaps the most distinguished, with the batting beginning to show real depth, and Frank Ford offering strong bowling support to Woods. Ford had come up from Repton with a reputation as an elegant, hard-hitting left-hander, but it was his slow left-arm bowling that was starting to flourish in his second year. He took five wickets in the Australians' first innings, and proved an admirable foil to Woods's pace, finishing the season with fourty-six victims to Sammy's sixty. Their bowling played a crucial part in all three victories that year, and in the win against Sussex they thrashed the southern county's hapless attack to the tune of 110 in only fifty minutes. Woods was brilliant in the Varsity Match, taking six for 48 in Oxford's only innings, but the weather had the final say. Despite an agreement to extend the match into a fourth day, the rain never relented long enough to allow Cambridge the victory it deserved, and the result was the first draw in the series for forty-four years. For once, Cambridge's outcricket had been outstanding, but in the Australian game there had been one reminder of how things had been only too recently. The powerful Percy McDonnell made a long hit down the ground, and George Kemp chased rather laboriously. On being told by a wag in the crowd to get on a bicycle, Kemp held the ball up while he told the gentleman what he thought of him, and meanwhile the batsmen ran seven!

The 1889 side was regarded by *Wisden* as a fair-weather side, strong on hard wickets, but liable to crumble on slow or wet ones. This was certainly borne out by the mixed results, which consisted of four wins, most of them through high scoring by Cambridge, and the same number of losses, three of them on difficult wickets. The innings of the season was by Ford, setting up a ten-wicket victory over Sussex with a brilliant 123 in less than two hours, and the match of the season was two days later against the MCC at Lord's. Cambridge reached the close of the second day precariously poised at 43 for four, chasing 171 to win, but next day Freeman Thomas, future MP for Hastings, set up a palpitating two-wicket win with a calmly compiled 61. The Varsity Match was a stroll in comparison, resulting in triumph for the Light Blues by an innings and 105 runs. The result had been predicted by many, and little excitement was created despite another superb display of fast bowling by Woods, who picked up eleven more wickets. It would take sterner opposition from Oxford to reveal just how good the team of this era really was.

SEVEN

THE END OF THE GOLDEN AGE

The start of cricket's 'Golden Age' is usually given, rather arbitrarily, as 1890, and it is said to have carried on until the outbreak of war in 1914. At Cambridge, it was more a question of a golden age coming to an end at the turn of the 1890s, but it was certainly a glorious end, seeing a flowering of talent almost as great as that of 1878. Indeed, if batting depth is anything to go by, the team of 1890–1891 has no equals, as with six top-class all-rounders to call on, Cambridge could afford to have Digby Jephson, later scorer of eleven first-class hundreds, coming in as last man. To be fair, Jephson was very lucky to gain a Blue three years in a row, as he showed no form with the bat, and hardly bowled for Cambridge. After leaving university, however, he became the Ovalites' favourite for his adoption of the ancient art of lob-bowling, and for his uncomplicated hitting and gentlemanly captaincy. Three other new recruits that proved of far greater immediate value were Arthur Hill, a gifted sportsman from Marlborough, Edward Streatfeild, a fast bowler from Charterhouse, and, rising above the pack, Harrow's own Stanley Jackson, for many the epitome of everything the 'Golden Age' stood for.

The decade could not have got off to a more dramatic start. The first game under Sammy Woods' captaincy was against C.I. Thornton's XI, and it turned out to be an extraordinary two days of cricket. Woods and Streatfeild, the latter on his debut, had the invitation team out for 68 on a damp pitch. Cambridge found the conditions almost as difficult, but managed a lead of 62. When Thornton's men went in again, Woods carried on where he had left off, taking six more wickets at the end of the first day. The next morning, he and MacGregor, firmly ensconced in their new lodgings, invited four of the opposition round for a hearty breakfast. On the menu were seven hot lobsters, bacon and eggs, and cold tongue, washed down with 'Jesus audit ale'. Not finding any takers for the lobsters, the hosts devoured them quite happily on their own, and, suitably fortified, Woods went on to devour some

Hon. F. S. Jackson (Yorkshire)

Stanley Jackson in his Red Rose days.

batsmen for afters. Bowling at his fastest and straightest, Sammy shot out the rest of the batting, ending up with all ten wickets himself, including seven clean bowled. The drama was not over yet, though. Needing only 72 to win, Cambridge faltered against the accuracy of Briggs and Mold, and, when the sixth wicket fell, 24 were still needed. Jackson, also on his debut, showed the cool head that was always to be a feature of his play, and the students got home without any further loss.

Woods' feat has never been repeated for Cambridge, and news of his heroics soon spread. Cyril Foley, who sat out this game but opened the batting in the next match, later recalled the words of the exasperated Master of Jesus College:

'I wish, Mr Woods… you were as proficient with your pen as you are with the cricket ball. I do not believe you know the meaning of the motto of this college, which you may notice is inscribed over the door.'

The motto in question was SEMPER EADEM (always the same). Woods looked up at it and said in his quiet drawl:

'Yes, I do, Mr Morgan, that's the menu.'

The 1890 side. Woods is sitting in the middle. C.P. Foley is sitting to his right with the kitten.

Woods also set an all-time Cambridge record with his match analysis of fifteen for 88, and even Mr Morgan was forced to forgive him his academic failings in the face of the universal awe in which Sammy was held.

Despite the team's strength in depth, Woods' true value was highlighted when, soon after the match, he strained his side and had to sit out the next three matches. The first two were lost by large margins, and only in the third match, against Yorkshire, did anyone step up to fill the breach. First, Hill and Streatfeild put on 101 for the last wicket to establish a lead of 136, and then Jackson took seven for 53 to leave a target of only 11, which was achieved for the loss of one wicket. With twelve wickets in the match, Jackson had secured his place in the eleven for a long time to come, and indeed never missed a match in his four years at Cambridge. His fast-medium bowling brought him second place in the Cambridge averages behind Woods in his first season, but his cultured and correct strokeplay was only to blossom in his last two years with the Club.

Woods was able to return for the visit of the Australian tourists, although he was not yet back to his best. The match was mainly notable for the heroic struggle by the batsmen to save the match after a first-innings deficit of 162. Only two of them failed to reach double figures, and Streatfeild, promoted two places to number nine, was still there on 74 when time ran out. He pulled off another epic performance in the next match at The Oval, when he took six for 34 and reduced Surrey to 72 for seven in pursuit of 147 to win. Again, time was called before a positive result could be achieved, but Cambridge made sure it had plenty of time in the next match, against Sussex. Indeed, so positively did the Cantabs bat that in the second innings they set up a new record score for English first-class cricket. Cambridge was 91 behind after the first knock, but Foley and MacGregor got together in a stand of 214 in 170 minutes to set a positive tempo. Ford and Hale carried

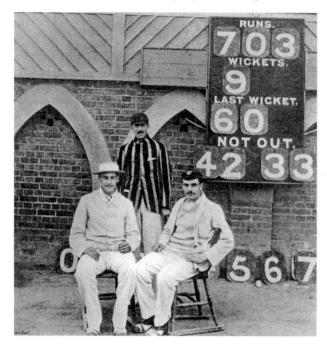

The scoreboard after Cambridge's record score, made against Sussex in 1890.

on to take the score to 494 for seven at the close of the second day, but if the Sussex bowlers thought that was it they were sadly mistaken. Next morning, 209 runs were added in only ninety minutes, with Ford leading the way with a brilliant 191 in two-and-a-half hours. Woods declared at 703 for nine, and Sussex held on until the last hour before finally capitulating, leaving Cambridge victors by the staggering margin of 425 runs.

After coming down to earth against the MCC, Cambridge proved its superiority in the Varsity Match, even though it was played in farcically wet conditions. Woods and Streatfeild were far too much for Oxford, bowling them out for 42 and 108; even so, they only just left enough time for the batsmen, as torrential rain started soon after the winning hit was made. Foley, very much a lesser mortal in this glittering line-up, had put on a vital 32 in the first innings with Jackson, and tells how Jackson:

hit a full pitch to square leg, narrowly missing the big clock which hung in the ivy on the old tennis court…

'Jacker, you nearly hit the clock', I said. 'Ah', said Jacker, looking round, 'I never thought of that.'

It was this kind of self-belief that summed up the amateur spirit of the age, certainly more than results, for there were still three defeats to set against the four victories, a record that meant the 1878 squad remained unchallenged as the greatest. Fortunately, the team would remain pretty much unchanged for another year, allowing it one last crack at immortality.

The Cambridge authorities allowed Woods a last year in the team, provided he relinquished the captaincy to MacGregor, who was also in his final season. The Freshmen's fixture was notable for the performance of Cyril Wells of Dulwich School, who opened both the batting and the bowling. As a result, Wells found himself in the first eleven for the first game of the season, a benefit match for the groundsman Walter Watts against C.I. Thornton's XI. Watts must have been pleased with both the strength of the opposition and the standard of play, as a ding–dong battle ended in feverish excitement with the visitors scraping home by one wicket. Two more defeats were followed by an exceptional sequence of victories against Yorkshire, Surrey and Sussex. Jackson took ten wickets against Yorkshire, Woods fourteen against Surrey, and the Sussex game was noteworthy for its high scoring, over 300 being scored in all four innings. Cambridge could approach the season's finale with confidence, having won three and lost four, while Oxford had won none and lost five. Woods again carried all before him, securing eleven more wickets, but Cambridge made a huge meal of the victory target of 90. Briefly, it looked as if Oxford's Berkeley would emulate Cobden twenty-one years before, as he bowled Streatfeild with 2 to make and then MacGregor with the scores level. The man for such a crisis was surely S.M.J. Woods, but he had not expected to have anything to do with it. With no time to don pads and gloves, he ran on, danced down the wicket to his first ball and drove it to the long-on boundary. Thus his Cambridge career ended, with the same style and flourish he had brought to it from day one.

Off the pitch, the Club was ready to take the next big step – buying the freehold of Fenner's. In 1889, Caius College, the Club's landlord, had taken back the orchard, which had been the only place to practise while a match was going on. Now, at a meeting of the Club on 26 October, the discussion was all about the improvements that Caius wanted to make. It intended to decrease the area of the ground, thus having a negative impact on gate receipts. The Club, together with the Athletic Club, saw only one option – to negotiate a price for the freehold. On 10 February 1892, the Bursar of Caius relayed to the Club the news that:

The Master and Fellows of Caius… were willing to sell for £12,000, to be paid by Michaelmas 1894, the land to be secured as an open space for ever, except as to certain specified parts, and on these parts no buildings save necessary offices or stands to be erected, the CUCC to surround the ground with a brick wall. Any part of the purchase-money, not exceeding £4,000, might remain on mortgage at 3½ per cent interest.

It was not until December that the proposal was formally accepted, and costs calculated. The Club had already begun fundraising. The total required was more like £12,800, £6,000 of which would come from the savings of the two Clubs, and the rest from voluntary subscriptions. It had raised £4,600 by this stage, and by January the original target had been exceeded, allowing the acquisition of other small plots of land next door to Fenner's. The transfer officially took place in November 1895, but the mortgage was rather more than planned at £7,500. With eleven acres to

Leslie Gay, a fine successor to MacGregor behind the stumps.

call its own, the Club had secured its future income and an opportunity to provide better practice facilities. With the MCC finally providing an annual subsidy of about £250, enough to cover the mortgage payments, and the Athletic Club continuing to run profitably, the books could more or less be balanced. Now it just needed the team's results to be in credit for everyone to be happy.

In the end, the record of the 1892 team might have been better than its immediate predecessor if it had not been for the unwarranted omission of one of the game's greatest ever talents. Kumar Shri Ranjitsinhji had come up to Cambridge in the autumn of 1888, hoping initially to win a Blue for tennis, but he increasingly rated his chances at cricket, a game in which he was untutored but that he practised assiduously. During 1892, Ranjitsinhji, or 'Smith' as he was known to start with because of the supposed difficulties of saying his name, scored over 2,000 runs in all matches and gained a huge following around Cambridge. Unfortunately, the Blues' captain, Stanley Jackson, was not one of his admirers. Jackson was a gentleman through and through, and a stickler for the orthodoxy that had been drilled into him on the playing fields of Harrow. Ranji may have stood more chance of being picked if Woods had still been captain, but under Jackson discipline and appearance were paramount. He did not trust the evidence of his own eyes when he saw the Indian batting on Parker's Piece, thinking that his methods were unsuitable for the rigours of first-class cricket, and the future Prince had to wait one more year for his chance. The truth was that in the Cambridge scene of the 1890s, fitting in was essential, and Ranji was excluded from the 'club' on two counts – his batting style was unorthodox, and, just as importantly, he was not white.

A PRINCE OF CRICKET.

Ranji, as seen by a contemporary cartoon.

Without Ranji, the Blues team won and lost the same number of games as in 1891, in large part due to the all-round brilliance of the captain, who topped both batting and bowling averages. The bowling was generally adequate, but the absence of Woods was keenly felt. His replacement, Hugh Bromley-Davenport, had on occasion been Jackson's nemesis in the Eton–Harrow match, but he failed to live up to his schoolboy reputation as a tearaway left-arm fast bowler. *Wisden* reported with a sigh:

We are forced to the conclusion that he lacks the stamina necessary for first-class cricket. If only his physical means were at all commensurate with his enthusiasm, he would long before this have taken a prominent position.

At least he looked the part, thus fitting in with Jackson's definition of everything that was right about the game and the Empire. Another who not only looked the part, but played it, was MacGregor's replacement as wicketkeeper, Leslie Gay. A most accomplished keeper, Gay also played in goal for the Corinthians and on three occasions for England. Since he also played in the famous First Test on Stoddart's 1894–95 Australian trip, he has the unique distinction of being both goalkeeper and wicketkeeper for England. Meanwhile, in 1892 he was selected to play for the Gentlemen against the Players, the ultimate accolade in the absence of Test matches that year, but was forced to decline.

Highlights of the season were the wins against Surrey and Sussex, in which Jackson and Streatfeild took thirty wickets between them, and there was no doubt that Cambridge was the favourite for the great occasion at Lord's at the end of June. When Oxford was 0 for two early on the first day, this confidence seemed thoroughly justified, and although Douglas Jardine's father Malcolm, and Ranji's future Sussex colleague C.B. Fry started a recovery, Cambridge was still in the ascendancy at 157 for five. The left-handed V.T. Hill then joined Jardine in a scintillating partnership of 178 in only 100 minutes, a sixth-wicket record for the fixture. After that the match was always beyond Cambridge's grasp, even though Streatfeild led a rally in the second innings with a stirring century. Jackson took three wickets in a lion-hearted effort to prevent an Oxford walkover, but the five-wicket winning margin was comfortable enough in the end. Perhaps Jackson's supreme confidence had boiled over into arrogance, but in the final analysis Cambridge had only been beaten by a magical passage of play, the quality of which has rarely been surpassed in the match's history.

Jackson's natural arrogance took a further knock in the winter of 1892–93, when he toured India with Lord Hawke's party of amateurs. What he saw there gave him a new-found respect for the cricketers of the subcontinent, and led indirectly to him picking Ranji for the first match of the new season. He was impressed by the dedication he showed in the nets both at Fenner's and Parker's Piece, and was struck by the remark of Bill Lockwood, the Surrey and England fast bowler who spent many hours bowling to the young Indian, that there were two or three worse batsmen in the Blues team. Given the impression that Ranji was making in the minds of so many good judges, Jackson could ignore him no longer. He made his debut against C.I. Thornton's XI batting at number eight, and immediately looked comfortable playing at this august level. His major contribution came in the sixth match, against the Australians, when he top-scored in both innings with 58 and 37 not out. The second-innings effort was particularly noteworthy, since it was made on a wearing pitch against an international attack, and it was enough for Jackson to promise him his Blue immediately after the game. The match was doubly significant historically, as it was also the first time in a first-class fixture that Ranji had unveiled his new-fangled stroke, the leg-glance.

The Australian game was a second successive loss for the students, interrupting a triumphant run of four straight victories against quality opposition. The bowlers were in particularly good form in the early games, Jackson taking a career best eight for 54 against A.J. Webbe's XI, and Wells, the one man who had championed Ranji's cause throughout, six for 36 against Yorkshire. Indeed, Wells was turning into something of a hero altogether. *Wisden* enthused:

In a normal season, Wells, bowling with the same degree of accuracy and skill, would certainly have taken a good many more wickets. Even on the hard grounds he could often make the ball do enough to beat the bat, and his pitch was always excellent. In a word, he was by far the best amateur slow bowler of the year.

As it was, he took an impressive fouty-seven wickets at the modest average of 13, while Jackson topped the batting with 649 runs at 43. His promise was at last fulfilled when he made his first century for the University against the MCC in two hours and five minutes. Just for good measure, he followed it in his very next innings with a chanceless 123 off the mighty Surrey attack, although it was not enough to prevent a sound defeat. Winning ways returned against Sussex, and emphatically so with an innings defeat of the MCC at Lord's. The omens were good for swift revenge over the old enemy in the last match of the season.

The Varsity Match turned out to be a dull affair, except for a controversial incident at the end of Oxford's first innings. In reply to Cambridge's 182, Oxford was poised to follow on at 95 for nine, the laws of the day only requiring a deficit of 80 for the batting side to be required to go in again. The two not-out batsmen had a mid-wicket conference, the purpose of which was clear – they were to attempt to throw their wickets away to ensure that Oxford did have to follow on. Cyril Wells immediately took matters into his own hands, bowling two balls to the boundary so that the follow-on was avoided. Until 1900, the follow-on was compulsory, and although at first sight there seems no reason why Cambridge should not have wanted Oxford to bat again, we can see that there was method in Wells' madness if we consider the circumstances surrounding the defeat by the Australians. In that game, Cambridge had established a first-innings lead of 94, but its bowlers tired as the Australians piled up runs at the second time of asking. Cambridge then collapsed

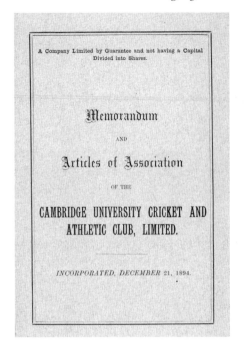

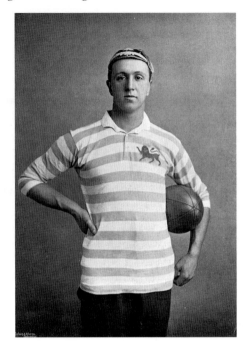

Above left: A new company was founded in 1894.

Above right: Frank Mitchell, one of many to be awarded a double Blue.

on a crumbling wicket, and this was exactly the scenario that Wells and Jackson were anxious to avoid here. Sure enough, Oxford was all out for 64 in the last innings as the wicket deteriorated, leaving Cambridge an ample victory margin of 266 runs. Although there was a brief furore in the press over the incident, Jackson stood by the tactic, and received support from no less a figure than W.G. Grace, never one to miss a trick on or off the pitch. Furthermore, the episode gave new life to the campaign to alter the follow-on law, and the first step was finally taken in 1895 when the margin was increased to 120 runs.

After such a continuous stream of talent for so many years, it was inevitable that there should be a backlash eventually, and it duly occurred in 1894. At one fell swoop, the successful attack from the previous campaign was removed, leaving a yawning gap that could not be filled in a hurry. This decline was reflected in the fact that two change bowlers, James Douglas and Frank Mitchell, topped the averages, and also in the results – only two wins and no less than seven losses in ten games. Mitchell was one of several new recruits, including the Druce brothers, Norman and Walter, who showed promise of better things to come, but didn't yet look like champions. Walter's initials were W.G., but it was *the* 'W.G.' that was determined that his progeny should not be ignored by the Cambridge selectors. W.G. Grace junior, or Bertie as he was known by the family, was a cricketer of moderate talent, and could not get into the team at the start of the season. His father therefore decided, rather unsubtly, to pick him for the MCC against the University at Fenner's, but his plan was foiled when Bertie got out for a duck. After junior had finally made his University debut against Sussex, W.G. *père* decided that there was still time for his son to gain a Blue in the last trial match, and duly selected him again to play for the MCC at Lord's. Although he took six Cambridge wickets, he was out for another first-innings duck, and even a second-innings 54 was not enough to sway the balance at the eleventh hour. W.G. senior gained some sort of revenge by dispatching the toiling student attack to all parts in a masterly knock of 196.

With or without the young Grace, Cambridge contributed little to a lacklustre game against Oxford, the chief distinction of which was a rather laboured hundred by C.B. Fry for the opposition. The Light Blues could only bide their time and hope for some more penetrative bowling in 1895. Sure enough, the good Lord provided in the form of fast bowlers Horace Gray and William Lowe, as well as the ambidextrous Clem Wilson. Gray was a product of Cambridge's Perse School, the first from that institution to gain a Blue for cricket. He did not play any further first-class cricket after graduation, devoting himself to the Church. Wilson, who would switch quite happily from right-arm medium-pace to slow left-arm in the course of an over, also gave up the game as soon as he was ordained, but not before he had toured South Africa with Lord Hawke in 1898, playing in two Tests without making a major contribution. This new trio took 114 wickets between them, and together with the prolific batting of the Druce brothers, brought about a considerable revival in the fortunes of the Club. The expanded fixture list of eleven games saw four wins mixed with four losses, and the chance for some brilliant individual feats. Mitchell started the season with 191 against Somerset, but he was trumped by Norman Druce, who scored three hundreds including a frustrating

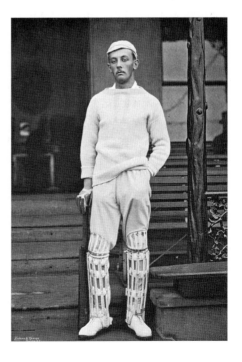

Norman Druce, a masterful batsman in the 1890s.

199 not out against the MCC. Bizarrely, he had made the same score batting for the Perambulators against the Etceteras (a quaintly named trial match) at the start of the season. Many years later, the old journalist Percy Piggott recalled of the MCC game:

The irony of it was that the last two wickets in the innings fell to consecutive deliveries before he could get the bowling... This was in the days before scores were telephoned to the news agencies at very frequent intervals as they are today; and I well remember the captain of the opposing side going to the scoring box at the close of the innings to make quite sure that Druce's score was correct, and on being informed that it had been very carefully checked he made the tentative suggestion that a single should be taken from the extras and added to Druce's total; but the scorers, quite rightly in my opinion, declined to rise to the bait.

Fortunately for Druce, it wasn't long before he had a chance to rectify matters, but for now there was the serious business of beating Oxford to address. Although he failed in both innings, his brother Walter led the batting with two fine displays. The Dark Blues were making a fair stab at chasing over 300 to win until Lowe intervened with a spell of three for 5 off twenty-two balls after lunch on the last day, hustling the dazed opposition to defeat by 134 runs.

While the team of the mid-1890s was undoubtedly a talented one, there was still room in its firmament for a real star, or at least an embryonic one. Gilbert Jessop's arrival in 1896 filled the vacancy perfectly, and over the next four years he was to achieve nearly as much as Jackson, while developing his reputation as an explosive entertainer *par excellence*. Jessop had already been playing for Gloucestershire for

The 'Croucher' poised to unwind.

two years by the time he came up to Christ's College, and so needed very little in the way of a trial to convince his captain, Frank Mitchell, of his value to the Club. Like Woods before him, he was no scholar, but he was at least member of a college known for its sporting dons. However, this sportsmanship was strained to the limit by the infrequency of Jessop's visits to chapel, and consequently he missed a chance of athletic glory when he was banned from leaving the college after nine o'clock during the week of the Varsity billiards match. On the field he got off to an unspectacular start in the traditional openers against C.I. Thornton's and A.J. Webbe's elevens, both of which resulted in heavy losses, but he made amends against Yorkshire, bowling at his fastest to take nine wickets in the match, and bolstering the lower order with a typically quickfire 47.

The rest of the summer was a tale of high scoring and controversy. The runs began to flow in the first match against the MCC, in which Ranjitsinhji made a brilliant hundred against his alma mater. For Cambridge, Cuthbert Burnup, fresh from his one England football cap – at outside left in a 2-1 defeat by Scotland – was especially unlucky not to make three figures, scoring 95 and 93. The game was drawn, but it was a good warm-up for the Sussex match, which as so often was an excuse for a student run-feast. Out of a total of 514, Mitchell scored 110, Jessop 93 and William Hemingway, a scholarly individual from Uppingham, his one and only first-class hundred. Sussex capitulated by an innings, but the MCC, whose attack was headed by Albert Trott and Fred Martin of Kent, was to provide rather sterner opposition in the return game at Lord's. At the end of an eventful first day, the MCC was 115 ahead in its second innings, and the next day its batsmen proceeded to put the match all but out of Cambridge's reach. Finally, the Cantabs were required to make 507 for victory, a seemingly forlorn task. Matters were even more desperate when the openers, Burnup and W.G. Grace junior, were removed for just 38, and the number three, Harold Marriott was forced to retire hurt. Trott was at his fieriest, and he made one get up and hit Marriott, much to the alarm of his captain. Mitchell protested vehemently, and Trott was taken off, temporarily depriving the MCC of its major strike force.

Much has been said of the farce that this made the game into, but in fact Trott resumed next day when the score was 98 for two, so the damage was limited in that respect. There must, however, have been some advantage to Druce and Wilson, who could now play themselves in against lesser pace, and they made full use of their chance. The third wicket did not fall until 280, and when Druce was out for 146, Marriott resumed his innings and took control. Wickets began to fall at regular intervals, and at 389 for seven the odds strongly favoured the MCC. Marriott, joined by a staunch ally in wicketkeeper Edward Bray, started to plunder the bowling mercilessly, and gradually the unthinkable was becoming the possible. These two saw Cambridge home by two wickets with a partnership of 118 in just seventy-five minutes, and an astonishing new record for a winning fourth-innings total had been created. Before this, no side had even scored as much as 400 to win in the last innings, and 507 was only beaten for the first time during the writing of this book, by Central Province of Sri Lanka, who scored 513 to win a match against

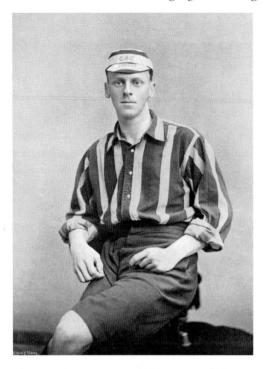

E.H. Bray, wicketkeeper in the 1890s.

Southern Province. The question mark remains as to whether the effort was worthy of the record, given that Mitchell, wanting to preserve his players from injury before the Varsity Match, had tried to dictate who should be allowed to bowl for the opposition. At this distance, it seems a typical example of the double standards of Victorian 'gentlemanly' behaviour – win at all costs while appearing to uphold the ideals of 'fair play' – and as such leaves a rather bitter taste.

Much more acceptable to modern mores was Cambridge's part in the central incident in the Varsity Match, but at the time it caused far more of a furore. Cambridge had made a solid start, rather too solid in the opinion of *The Times*, which complained of the scoring rate of 'only' 58 an hour. In reply to Cambridge's 319, Oxford had reached 5 for no wicket at the end of the first day, but wickets fell steadily all through the next, and at 133 for eight, the 200 needed to avoid the follow-on seemed a long way off. However, the ninth-wicket pair of Hartley and Cunliffe gradually closed the gap, until Hartley was brilliantly caught by Marriott off Wilson. The last man, Lewis, was known as something of a rabbit, and it seemed certain that Oxford would indeed have to follow on. Just as Jackson had been in 1893, Mitchell was faced with a perverse law that gave the fielding captain no discretion to waive the follow-on, and therefore, with 12 still needed to save it, Mitchell instructed fast bowler Eustace Shine to bowl three balls, two of which were no-balls, to the boundary. Shine then bowled Cunliffe with the score on 202, and so Cambridge did not have to bowl again. What happened next is best described in the words of one of the participants, Plum Warner of Oxford:

On returning to the pavilion the Cambridge Eleven were hooted at by the members of the MCC, and in the pavilion itself there were angry scenes, many members losing all control over themselves. Winged words were given and returned, Cantab was divided against Cantab, and brother against brother... Lord Cobham supported Mitchell, and his brother, Edward Lyttelton, condemned him.

The Light Blues were said to be affected by the demonstrations, and certainly young W.G. completed a 'pair' in front of the 'Grand Old Man' of cricket, who had striven so hard to ensure that Bertie, somehow, got to Lord's. But not only he suffered from this malaise – soon five more of his teammates were back in the pavilion with only 61 on the board. Druce then played beautifully for 72, his highest score in the Varsity Match, and, with the help of Bray's 41, he managed to set Oxford a challenging target of 330. Neither side had ever scored anything like this total in the fourth innings of the match, and at lunch time on the last day there seemed little likelihood of this changing. Oxford had lost three wickets for 60, but then G.O. Smith, the greatest centre forward of his day, displayed another of his sporting talents in a brilliant innings of 132. The middle order stood firm in support, and in the end victory was achieved with surprising ease by four wickets. It must have seemed poetic justice that Oxford should triumph after Cambridge had caused such controversy, but really Mitchell had only done what any captain would have, in the face of such a farcical situation. Moving at its usual snail's pace, the MCC finally changed the law in 1900, but only after a further occurrence had prevented England

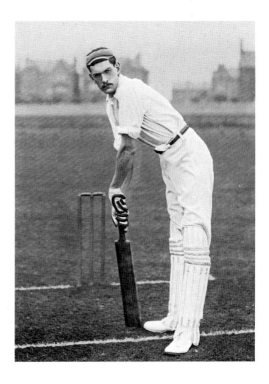

W.G. Grace junior, not known for inheriting his father's style.

from winning the Old Trafford Test of 1899. At least CUCC could not be accused of being behind the times – ladies were admitted to the pavilion at Fenner's for the first time in 1896!

The esteem in which Cambridge University was held at this juncture was reflected by *Wisden* in 1898, when it selected Druce and Jessop as two of its cricketers of the year – a considerable coup for two players at the beginning of their careers. Admittedly, Jessop achieved a lot for Gloucestershire in 1897, but Druce's feats were almost entirely for Cambridge. He comfortably topped the Club's averages, scoring 726 runs at an average of 66, and winning the following plaudits from the cricketers' Bible:

He is a delightful batsman to look at, his style being a model of freedom… He plays his own game… scoring on the on-side from straight balls in a fashion only possible to a batsman with a genius for timing.

Druce had done enough over the last three seasons to convince the selectors to send him to Australia under A.E. Stoddart, and he played in all five Tests without really distinguishing himself. Meanwhile, however, he had started the Cambridge season sensationally, setting a new individual record for the Club with an innings of 227 not out against C.I. Thornton's XI. With Jessop and Shine now joined by Eton's slow left-armer Herman de Zoete, Druce had a formidable attack to back up his captaincy, and there were always enough runs from the likes of Burnup, Mitchell and Wilson. The only blots in Cambridge's copybook this year were two losses to Sussex, but otherwise the season was a long triumphal march, with seven wins and a wet draw in the other fixtures. Jessop managed forty-one wickets and 462 runs, including his first century for Cambridge, which came against the touring Philadelphians. Although possessing a reasonable attack, including the legendary J.B. King, on this occasion the conditions rendered it rather more friendly than normal, as Jessop relates:

One of the mainstays of their bowling was H.P. Baily, a short, squat, bespectacled figure, whose aspect as he delivered the ball was one of cheery optimism… He was a most generous-minded man and his gift of half-volleys deserves to be recorded. Even after one of these had found the road outside the entrance gate of Fenner's his optimism did not leave him, and as the boundary at the other end looked longer he asked George Patterson if he might reverse ends… with the result that the very first ball disappeared over the wall into the grounds of a girls' school.

In all, Jessop batted just ninety-five minutes for his 140, hitting two sixes clean out of the ground, and twenty-one fours. Percy Piggott happened to be one of the spectators, and as he records, Jessop:

made five or six big drives which landed in Walter Watts' garden alongside the pavilion. Watts had a bed of asparagus of which he was justly proud, and which at this particular time of the year was just in full crop. I happened to remark to Watts on the brilliance of Jessop's hitting. Watts, in his quiet, dour way, replied 'If he does it many more times he'll spoil my asparagus.'

Here was Jessop's first warning – in future, it would not just be harmless summer vegetables that got a bruising, but bowlers' egos the length and breadth of the land.

Following the excitement of 1896, the Varsity Match was a strangely muted affair, although Cambridge won without looking convincing. Jessop's contribution of six wickets and 42 in eighteen minutes was the only one to raise the pulses, and this seemed to set the tone for the rest of the century. Druce was sorely missed, and Wilson's 100 in a losing cause in the Varsity Match of 1898, along with a brilliant 171 not out by Jessop, were the only highlights of a dull couple of years. The latter innings was made out of a total of only 246 in the Yorkshire match of 1899, and took less than two hours to compile. As captain, however, Jessop failed to add to his reputation, and his bowling was handicapped all season by a strained side. The plain fact was that the students of this period were not good enough to bowl the opposition out twice on increasingly true pitches, as was highlighted by the Varsity Match. For the first time, the game was drawn without any intervention from the weather, starting a trend for unfinished clashes that has continued ever since. If this was a sign of things to come, a verse composed in honour of Jessop's brevity of length as a bowler was even more prescient:

> *There was a young Fresher named Jessop,*
> *Who was pitching 'em less and less up,*
> *Until one of the pros*
> *Got a blow on the nose,*
> *Said, 'In a helmet of brass – I'll dress up.'*

EIGHT

IN DECLINE

As a new, confident age dawned, the cricketing landscape of Cambridge seemed to be the same as ever – a settled fixture list, an imposing pavilion, a thriving college system and a fleet of professional bowlers, ready to bowl to any member for the small consideration of a shilling for half an hour. Unfortunately, on a closer inspection, things were not so rosy. The quality of practice available in the nets merely covered up for the fact that there were no students who could bowl anything like as well as the professionals, and, although the batting was adequate, the Fenner's wicket had become so poor that there were never enough runs to bowl at anyway.

Under the stewardship of Yorkshire's Tom Taylor, the University had a wretched start to the century, winning only two of its eleven games. The fact that it only lost two was purely due to the weather, for out of the remaining seven games, the students were lucky to escape defeat in five of them. The wins were against weak MCC sides, but the first one at least threw up a remarkable performance from the slow left-armer Lancelot Driffield, who took seven for 7 in forty balls in the premier club's second innings. Having come from nowhere, he faded rapidly back into obscurity, finishing the season with only fourteen wickets altogether. He did have the consolation of keeping goal for the University for three years in succession. The only other noteworthy feat was the dashing John Daniell's hundred in two-and-a-quarter hours against Surrey. Daniell had already played rugby for England, and would captain Somerset in the best amateur spirit, but as a cricketer he was not a serious replacement for the likes of Jessop.

After such a build up, it was not surprising that the Varsity Match started so badly for Cambridge. Taylor lost the toss and saw the Dark Blues pile up an unprecedented score on a perfect pitch. R.E. Foster played a supreme innings of 171 in just 190 minutes, setting a new record for the match in the process, and by the close of the first day, Oxford had reached an impregnable 480 for eight. The final total of 503 was another new record that stood for ninety-six years, but to its credit Cambridge also made full use of the conditions. The top nine all reached double figures, the highest score being Taylor's 74, and after the follow-on had been saved a draw seemed the only likely result. Cambridge reached the close in the second innings with eight wickets, and its pride, still intact. The one area in which the Cantabs definitely excelled was the fielding, with Daniell outstanding at point. However, from now on, if either team was to force a result on the benign pitches at headquarters, some new, penetrative bowlers would have to be unearthed from somewhere. There was no immediate sign of this happening at Fenner's or The Parks.

Not to put too fine a point on it, Cambridge was becoming a two or three-man band rather than the ensemble that it had been for so many years. Its leader in 1901, Sam Day, was fit to rank with some of those illustrious names, but he and Edward Dowson were the only two virtuoso performers in this outfit. Day was a batsman of exceptional eye and wristwork, and Dowson was described by *Wisden* as 'the best forcing player on the on-side seen at Cambridge since F.S. Jackson was in residence'. Not only that, he carried the bowling as well, taking fifty-two wickets with his slow left-armers, although he was well supported by the varied slow-medium of Rockley Wilson, younger brother of Clem. Wilson's batting style, the epitome of solidity, also complemented Dowson's. Having scored a century on his first-class debut, playing for A.J. Webbe's XI against the University in 1899, it was fitting that Rockley finally made his maiden hundred for Cambridge in the 1901 Varsity Match. The Wilsons thereby became the first brothers to have scored a century in the big match for Cambridge, emulating the feat of the Foster brothers for Oxford. Rockley had to wait nearly two decades for England recognition, having spent a memorable time as games master at Winchester. Some useful performances for Yorkshire in the summer holidays of 1920 convinced the desperate selectors that he should tour Australia that winter, and although he didn't disgrace himself, he was clearly not the future of English cricket at the age of forty-one.

Worcestershire was a new first-class county, and therefore it was not surprising that it was Cambridge's only scalp of the season. Typically, the major contributors to the win were Dowson's 97 and Wilson's fourteen for 75, but even their efforts couldn't prevent eight defeats in the warm-up matches. The only draw, against Yorkshire, featured an innings of 150 in four-and-a-half hours by the Etonian Henry Longman. It promised much, but turned out to be a flash in the pan – by the end of the season Longman was struggling to retain his place, and never played for Cambridge again after the Varsity Match. The great game itself was a close but not especially exciting affair, the tone being set by Wilson's worthy four-hour hundred. Dowson livened things up with his second innings, 70 in seventy-five minutes, but even so Day's declaration was over-cautious. Left a little over three hours to make 349 to win, the game seemed to be up for Oxford at 145 for seven with the light bad and forty minutes still left. At this point, Frank Hollins, who had batted number three in the first innings, joined the opener Cloudesley Marsham. Before getting off the mark, Hollins edged a ball from Peter Johnson into the slips, where it was

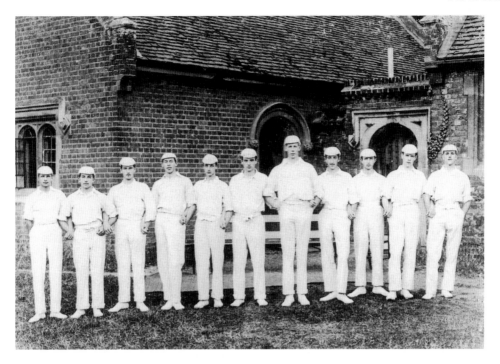

The Eton chorus line of 1899. Cambridge's H.K. Longman is fifth from the left.

apparently caught by Wilson. He threw the ball up and claimed the catch, but it could not be given out as the view of both umpires had been obscured. After that, Oxford successfully played out time, and Cambridge showed there were no hard feelings by helping Marsham reach his century before the close.

Despite 1902 being one of the wettest summers on record, the wickets at Fenner's, which had come under fire for several years, showed a considerable improvement after marl and loam were spread on them in the close season. The firmer wickets encouraged strokeplay, and enabled Cambridge to be more competitive than it had been for five years. Dowson's all-round contribution was again massive − 637 runs at an average of 33, and sixty-five wickets at 18. Wilson was also at his best with fifty-four wickets at 16, and he was able to captain the side to four victories, as against four losses and three defeats. Two new stars seemed to have been unearthed when Charles Ebden and Kenneth Fry, who had scored 100 and 95 not out respectively in trial matches, both made centuries in the season's opener against Leveson-Gower's XI. It was Ebden's first-class debut, but Fry, cousin of the great C.B., had already played for Sussex. Although Fry proved himself a competent wicketkeeper, neither he nor Ebden repeated their early success with the bat, although the latter made an impressive fifty against the Australians, before the students collapsed to an abject 46 all out in the second innings. However, they managed to wreak some havoc themselves, twice getting W.G. Grace's London County out for 73. On the first occasion, at Fenner's, the match ended in a draw, but the return at Crystal Palace resulted in a convincing win. Eric Penn took three for 4 and made some useful runs, smashing the top window of the refreshment room in the process. Penn was unique in that he had just returned from two years in the Boer War, having played for the University in 1899. Consequently, the committee passed a special regulation allowing him to resume his place in the side.

Dowson's major heroics for the season were against Surrey. He scored 71 not out and 50, and took three for 47 and eight for 68, thus becoming only the second Cambridge player after Walter Money in 1868 to achieve the match double of 100 runs and ten wickets. He also helped his teammates to a dramatic 44-run victory. Wilson also showed his class with 142 in 210 minutes against the MCC at Lord's, but he was powerless to prevent an innings defeat after his bowlers had conceded the small matter of 607. Fortunately, all three of the star names were on song when it mattered – against Oxford. The first two days belonged to the Dark Blues, but only just. Dowson and Wilson had taken eighteen wickets between them, and scored useful runs; now it was Sam Day's turn. Cambridge was given most of the final day to score 272, a stiff but not unobtainable target. Despite some anxiety when the score stood at 197 for five, Day made a nonsense of it, all bowlers coming alike as he compiled an assured unbeaten 117 in three-and-a-quarter hours. With him at the end was James Gilman, whose reminiscences of playing with W.G. for London County were captured for posterity by *Wisden* just before he died in 1976 at the age of ninety-seven.

Sam Day, captain in 1901.

With the departure of Day and Wilson, *Wisden* was forced to acknowledge that, apart from Dowson, who had been nominated captain, there was in 1903 'no cricketer on the side of more than quite ordinary ability'. Dowson's batting was exceptional, with 854 runs at 47 being a fitting swansong for his Cambridge career. However, his three hundreds were the only ones recorded by the team all season, and his bowling suffered through the lack of a suitable partner to replace Wilson. Three wins were small compensation for six heavy losses, although the match against Sussex was quite sensational. Sussex had a first-innings lead of just 4, and set Cambridge the unlikely victory target of 322. That the University achieved it with two wickets to spare was largely due to a third-wicket stand of 200 between Dowson and F.B. Wilson, later a famous sports journalist, but for now content to play the innings of his life in support of his captain. He also batted courageously in the second innings of the Varsity Match, but to no avail as Cambridge collapsed twice in the face of the multi-talented W.H.B. Evans.

Wilson succeeded Dowson at the helm for 1904, but a change of personnel made no difference to the playing record, which was even worse. At least Wilson could again call upon a reliable pair of bowlers in Harold McDonell and Guy Napier. Napier had arrived from Marlborough with a great reputation, and he did not disappoint with fifty wickets in his first season. McDonell was not far behind with forty-eight. The importance of these two to the side was amply demonstrated when Sussex rattled up 558 against Cambridge when both were absent. For once, the main problem was scoring enough runs, although Meyrick Payne announced himself as an aggressive opener by scoring 102 not out in just seventy-five minutes against the MCC. Only a brilliant innings by Ranjitsinhji, batting at number nine, enabled the latter to pull off an exciting victory. Perhaps this sense of being robbed was in Wilson's mind when he declared late on in the Varsity Match, setting Oxford a massive 495 to win in five-and-a-half hours. The main reason for the delay, though, was to allow the twenty-nine-year-old John Marsh the chance to beat R.E. Foster's series record. He duly reached 172 after a painstaking five-hour innings, and Wilson immediately declared. At 128 for six Oxford looked dead and buried, but Evans stood firm and the game was eventually called off in the gathering gloom. Much was made of Cambridge sacrificing victory for an individual, and unworthy record, but in reality three missed catches probably made all the difference, especially as two of them were off Evans. Nevertheless, the game had done nothing to remove the aura of negativity that was beginning to surround the ancient fixture.

Help was at hand, though, in the form of a classic clash in 1905 that restored faith in the adventurous nature of amateur cricket. Cambridge had had a disastrous build-up, winning only one of its preliminary matches while incurring four heavy losses. On the plus side, the captain Eric Mann saved the first match of the season with a magnificent 157, and Payne continued to strike fear into the opposition with spasmodically electrifying performances such as his 178 against Surrey. Best of all, Alfred Morcom came up from Repton to partner Napier, and a batsman of genuine quality was found in Morcom's former teammate, Dick Young. Young's trademark

Dick Young became captain in 1908, having kept wicket for England the previous winter.

was his thick spectacles, which he wore while playing cricket and amateur football for England. Naturally enough for a person with such thick glasses, he became a mathematics teacher at Eton and used his logical brain to continue theorising about cricket. One product of this was a pamphlet urging the lawmakers to allow captains the right to pour 100 gallons of water on any part of the pitch, an idea that never really caught on.

Despite new blood on both sides, the events of the first day at Lord's did not inspire any confidence that the previous year's contest might be improved upon. Cambridge scraped together a score of just over 200, and Oxford seemed destined for something equally mediocre at 99 for four. Raphael and Wright then put on 191, still a fifth wicket record for the match, and so Oxford managed to establish a lead of 101. Two hours later, Cambridge was 77 for six, still requiring 24 to make Oxford bat again. Just as in 1870, when the game seemed equally lost, an individual stepped forward to grab the game by the scruff of the neck. This time it was Leonard Colbeck, an inconsistent but talented performer, who was lost at sea in 1918 on the HMS *Ormonde* as it rounded the Cape of Good Hope. Unlike his fellow students of the preceding years, he was prepared to take risks, and certainly did so now:

Straight balls were cut behind point and went to the boundary like a flash, and it was impossible to place the field for his off-drive, since no man could say what ball he would select as a suitable medium for the exploitation of it.

Colbeck and McDonell added 143 in eighty-five minutes, allowing Mann to set a respectable target of 164. The game was evenly poised overnight, with Oxford 15 for three after a reshuffle of the batting order. Napier and Morcom made short work of the remaining batting on the third day, and in the end the victory margin was a relatively comfortable 40. Colbeck's brilliance had made it all possible, but the real difference between the teams was Cambridge's opening bowlers. In their three years at Lord's they took forty-seven of the sixty Oxford wickets to fall, and were the architects of victory in each of those years. Napier was perhaps the more impressive on all wickets, making the ball go away with his arm, and occasionally causing it to break back, a combination that was enough to earn grudging praise from *Wisden*, which described him as 'one of the steadiest and most dependable of amateur bowlers – not perhaps very difficult but always accurate and hard to score from'. Morcom particularly enjoyed bowling from the Pavilion End at Lord's, as it assisted his break back, and he never seemed to be quite the same bowler elsewhere. However that may be, in the game that mattered Cambridge had the ascendancy for the moment, and it also had its best opening attack since the days of Jackson and Woods.

With eight old Blues in residence, and fast bowler Percy May providing strong support to Napier and Morcom, 1906 was the most successful season since 1897. The six wins included a 305-run drubbing of Yorkshire, an innings defeat of Northamptonshire, and a successful chase against Surrey. In the latter match, the University was set 298 to win, and coasted home by eight wickets, mainly thanks to Payne's 128 out of 186 in only ninety minutes. The Yorkshire game was notable for an innings of 153 by the new captain, Charles Eyre, who had been a somewhat strange choice for the post after averaging 10 the year before. He played only one more first-class match after leaving Cambridge, and, by a macabre coincidence, both he and Napier were killed in action near Loos on exactly the same day, 25 September 1915. At least they knew the joy of victory against a different enemy, and one that was far more easily achieved.

Cambridge made all the running in the Varsity Match from Payne's explosive opening to Napier's final wicket. Payne scored the first 45 runs from the bat in fifteen minutes, taking 34 from two overs by Udal. He reached his 50 in twenty-five minutes, and when the fireworks came to an end, he had made 64 out of 73 in half an hour, with fourteen fours and only one single. The icing on Payne's cake was provided by the seven dismissals he took behind the stumps, creating a new record for Cambridge in these matches. His partner, Dick Young, had been almost strokeless in their opening stand, but as the innings progressed he accelerated, until he was last out for 150, made in 275 minutes with twenty-two fours. Eyre was able to declare early on the last day, leaving Oxford 422 to win. At 237 for nine humiliation seemed certain, but Curwen and Martin saved some face with a rollicking last-wicket stand of

90 in fifty-five minutes. *Wisden* memorably opined of Martin: 'There was no science in his batting, but an abundance of pluck'. Oxford still turned out plucky losers by 94 runs, and Cambridge could be satisfied that it had played hard and entertained throughout the summer. Indeed, if it had not been for an appalling epidemic of dropped catches, an unbeaten run would have been a distinct possibility.

By a remarkable coincidence, 1907 began with the captain scoring a century in the opening game for the third successive year. This time it was Meyrick Payne, who scored 129 in 145 minutes to set up an innings victory against Lancashire. The match was also notable for the debut of Charles Frederick Lyttelton, son of Charles George Lyttelton and grandson of the fourth Lord Lyttelton. The dynasty therefore became the first to have three successive generations of cricketers in the Cambridge team, a feat only subsequently equalled by the Doggart family. Charles junior announced himself with seven wickets in the match, but his form fell away, and he had to wait until 1908 for his Blue. Payne had a lot of bad luck with unavailability of key players due to exams and injuries, and only managed one more win before the Varsity Match, compared with four losses. The first day of the game itself was wet and cold, restricting the crowd to a comparatively small 8–9,000, and Napier and Morcom were able to bowl unchanged through an innings of frequent interruptions. Oxford managed an inadequate 141, but as the wicket worsened Cambridge struggled to stay in the match. Oxford had a lead of 33, but it failed to capitalise, and in the end Cambridge's target was only 146. Young and John Buchanan, a reliable batsman from Charterhouse, saw them to victory by five wickets, although if Oxford had not dropped Buchanan twice things may have been a lot tighter. The heroes were Napier and Morcom yet again, and at the end of their student careers they could look back on some remarkable achievements: in four games against Oxford, Napier had taken thirty-one wickets, while Morcom had twenty-one in three.

Young and Buchanan were to feature in prominent roles again, being captain in 1908 and 1909 respectively, but, despite leading by example, the lack of adequate replacements for Napier and Morcom meant that they could not conjure up any magic from their troops. Lyttelton's form picked up in 1908, and he was rewarded for his perseverance with fourty-three wickets. He was assisted by Eric Olivier, a South African-born Reptonian, who took fifty-four wickets with his fashionable 'swerve', another name for the swing bowling that had recently been developed by Yorkshire's George Hirst. However, they had no support at all, and the batting was weakened by the loss of Payne. Two future England players, Frank Mann and Neville Tufnell, made their entrances but their contribution was negligible, and they did not make the Varsity Match. This turned out to be one of the closest games of the series, with very little to choose between the teams throughout. In the final act, Oxford's Teesdale was out with the scores tied and two wickets left, but there were to be no Cobden-style heroics from Cambridge. The winning run was made at 6.40 p.m., but only just in time – torrential rain began only minutes later.

Another new prodigy was found in 1909 in the shape of John Bruce-Lockhart, an uncommonly slow leg-break bowler from Sedbergh who also represented the Cambridge and Scotland rugby teams at fly half. *Wisden* assessed his methods as follows:

Pitching his leg-breaks very high in the air, he met with great success against batsmen who jumped out to hit him; but he was so slow that the players who waited until the ball had pitched did not find him difficult.

Even so, he managed to bamboozle enough batsmen to claim fourty-nine victims in seven matches, including thirteen Yorkshiremen in the first game of the season. He was greatly assisted in his endeavours by the newly promoted Tufnell, who pulled off seven stumpings off his bowling, including five in the second innings. That match was the only victory recorded in a programme truncated by the weather, although a memorable run-chase against Sussex ended in a defeat by just 8 runs. The Varsity Match was once again frequently interrupted by rain, and Cambridge was lucky to escape with a draw after Oxford dithered over its declaration on the last day. There were only five-and-a-half hours playing time left at the start of the day, which should have been ample to push for victory. However, the closure did not come until four o'clock, leaving Cambridge 276 to make in two-and-three-quarter hours. Cambridge could do little except survive, a task made far simpler when the rain came once again. Bruce-Lockhart emerged with nine wickets, but he was never to have the same impact again; just like Olivier's swerve in 1909, once the secret of the party trick had been exposed, no one was baffled by it any more. But it had been fun while it lasted.

Frank Mann captained England in South Africa in 1922/23.

NINE

IN HIBERNATION

Even at their best, they were no more than just an average side. Nothing in their cricket, except perhaps Tufnell's wicket-keeping, was first rate.

Such was *Wisden's* verdict on Cambridge's 1910 outfit, and its accuracy was again underlined by a mediocre set of results under the stewardship of Michael Falcon. Wins against Surrey, Yorkshire and a weak Gentlemen's side were more than offset by five defeats, three of which were at home. In the latter match, Tufnell showed that he was not just a top-class stumper by becoming the first Cantabrigian to score a century before lunch on the first day of a match. This proved the high point of the summer, the nadir of which was reached when the batting subsided against Kent to be all out for just 45 on a sticky wicket.

Talking of collapses, the Australian Philip Le Couteur was instrumental in causing a procession in both innings of the Varsity Match with his mixture of leg-breaks and googlies, highlighting Cambridge's 'awkward weakness for playing forward', according to *Sporting Life*. Only the captain and the reliable New Zealander David Collins managed to reach double figures in both innings as Cambridge lost a hopelessly one-sided affair by an innings and 126 runs. Things looked so different when Le Couteur came to the wicket in Oxford's innings after the erratic but fast Alexander Cowie had helped reduce the old enemy to 30 for four. By the end of a rain-affected first day, he was already 94 not out, and he accelerated next day to reach 160 in 200 minutes with fifteen fours. If the truth be told, it was not one of the classic innings, as he was dropped four times and frequently edged through the slips. However, it could not have come at a more crucial time, and added to his eleven wickets for 66 it can safely be said that there has never been a greater all-round performance for either side in this venerable series of matches.

Le Couteur was at it again in 1911, taking another eleven wickets to spoil what was otherwise a vastly better season for Cambridge. Once again, Oxford seemed

Fenner's in about 1911.

to be on the rack when John Ireland, an all-rounder from Marlborough, took a hat-trick that included the wicket of Harry Altham, the future doyen of cricket historians. It recovered sufficiently to post a respectable total that Cambridge only bettered by 14, and then managed to set a tricky 315 to win. Le Couteur's eight for 99 saw to it that this was never likely, despite Frank Mann finally showing some of the form that made him England captain just over a decade later. Ireland was criticised both for taking himself off immediately after taking his hat-trick and for not picking Bruce-Lockhart, who had regained some of the form of two seasons before. Since only a few runs were scored after Ireland came off, the first criticism is a little harsh, but there was no doubt that the bowling would have benefited from the variety that Bruce-Lockhart brought to the game.

If one bowler was underused, another one was making up for a lot of lost time. Michael Falcon had hitherto been almost purely a batsman, but now he suddenly stepped forward as a fast bowler of immense promise. Writing in 1943, E.H.D. Sewell included Falcon in his all-time Cambridge University Eleven, and waxed lyrical about his bowling:

Falcon had an ideal high action, did not reduce his value by checking at delivery, and had good command at pitching the away-swerve where the batsman does not like it to pitch, i.e. if missed by the bat the ball will hit the wicket, and not too often the wicketkeeper. Owing to his pace and action he was also able to produce that highest proof of good fast bowling, the good length ball that gets up sharply.

Coupled with his batting, Falcon was now an impressive all-rounder, and he must have only narrowly missed England selection because of his infrequent appearances in first-class cricket. His life's work lay elsewhere, including a stint as MP for East Norfolk, but he still had time to become a legend on the Minor Counties circuit with Norfolk.

The Varsity Match took the gloss off an otherwise vastly improved performance, with only three other losses and no less than six wins to celebrate. The batting depth was the most pleasing feature, but a lack of fight against fast bowling was revealed by two losses to Surrey on lively wickets. The Irish Etonian, the Honourable Henry Mulholland, emulated Tufnell's feat of the year before by scoring 153 before lunch against the touring All-India team, the first from that country. In the process, he added a new Cambridge record of 259 for the first wicket with the New Zealander David Collins, but the real highlight was provided near the start of the season against Sussex. After following-on 158 behind, Cambridge showed much more backbone with a second effort of 437, led by a century from Falcon. Eric Kidd, captain in 1912, routed the Sussex batting, taking a career-best eight for 49 with his leg-spin, and pulling off a dramatic 42-run victory. As so often with these two rivals, the return match was also a humdinger. Sussex was set just 91 to win in the last innings, but collapsed to 67 for nine, before squeezing home by one wicket after half past seven. There was never a dull moment when Cambridge was in town.

Rain played havoc with the first-class fixture list in 1912, including the first and last ever Triangular Tournament between England, Australia and South Africa. It was not a great success, and hence was not repeated, but it did at least mean that Fenner's was honoured by two overseas visitors in the same season. Although Cambridge was not an outstanding side, it had an exceptional leader in Kidd, regarded as the best tactician at the University since the era of the Lytteltons. There was also the first appearance of another future England captain to make note of. The Honourable Freddie Calthorpe, uncle of Henry Blofeld, later led England in the first ever Tests played in the Caribbean, but for many years was a genuine all-rounder for Warwickshire. He announced himself on the Cambridge scene with figures of four for 12 against Middlesex, which helped to wrap up a win in the first match of the season. In the next, against Sussex, he scored 78 batting at number nine, while Kidd compiled an elegant 167. This game was also won, as was the next against Yorkshire, but the next victories had to wait for the end of the season trip to Lord's. Both the tourist matches were played on spiteful wickets, which led to an innings defeat by South Africa and a soggy draw against the Aussies.

Calthorpe again showed off his all-round ability against the Free Foresters, a fixture accorded first-class status for the first time. His contribution was 74 and four for 9, but his colleagues were thwarted by a storming knock of 152 not out by old Blue Norman Druce, still capable at the age of thirty-seven of showing the young upstarts a thing or two. The MCC match was a close affair, only won by two wickets in the end thanks to a breezy 72 by Reginald Lagden. He was in form in the season's finale against Oxford, hitting a timely 61 that left the scores tied on first innings. Luckily for Cambridge, G.E.V. Crutchley, whose 99 not out had held together Oxford's faltering first attempt, was absent with a bout of measles for the second innings. This left the stage clear for Reginald's brother Ronald Lagden, who chipped in with 68 and then bowled his brother before the close of the second day as Cambridge set off in pursuit of 214. Although the wicket was beginning to misbehave, some controlled aggression by Mulholland and Kidd in a fourth-wicket stand of 103 saw the Light Blues home by three wickets soon after lunch.

Mulholland was rewarded with the captaincy in 1913, and he was fortunate enough to inherit a very settled side. Ten Blues were already in residence, and there was a comforting solidity about the batting order. Kidd was in exceptional form, scoring 866 at an average of 72, and prompting *Wisden's* typically ambivalent comment: 'In his own way he is a very fine player'. Lagden was also prolific with 838 runs at 55, and the whole side made hay against a weak MCC attack, scoring 609 for eight declared to create a new record for Lord's. Nothing else of real note emerged from the season, and Cambridge came to the Oxford match needing to improve on a record of three wins and five losses. As it transpired, only five old Blues were selected, one notable absentee being the fast bowler Edward Baker, who had taken seven wickets in 1912. Mulholland judged, correctly as it turned out, that the Freshman left-arm spinner John Naumann would be more useful on a slow wicket. The choice was an inspired one; Naumann took eight wickets and along with Lagden, who made 71 and 45, proved to be the difference between the two teams as Cambridge

John Naumann played for Cambridge before and after the First World War.

won another tight match by four wickets. Unfortunately, Alfred Lyttelton did not get to see it, as he died two days before the start of the game. His memorial service was marked at twelve o'clock on the second day when the flags were lowered to half-mast, and players and spectators stood in silence for two minutes.

The last season before the First World War was not blessed with a single win against the counties, but there were some exciting moments against the invitation sides. The best of them was an astonishing tour de force by John Morrison, whose style, according to *Wisden*, had previously been 'marred by an exaggerated straddle' as he stood at the wicket. Now he was much better to look at, and much more potent. Having already scored 231 in a senior's trial match, he launched a withering assault on the MCC's hapless attack. In just 165 minutes he belted 233 not out, including thirty fours and four sixes in a seemingly ceaseless stream of shots. It was a new record for both Fenner's and Cambridge, and into the bargain he put on 255 for the third wicket with Mulholland. Morrison's second hundred came in a mere forty-five minutes, and it enabled a declaration that left the MCC with a huge task. It was less than equal to it, and for once the bowlers had an easy time of it, Calthorpe and Geoff Davies taking four wickets apiece. Davies was a medium-pacer who had some brief success with Essex, and took 45 wickets for Cambridge in 1914 at just under fifteen. It was to be his last summer – a year later he lost his life on the fields of France.

Davies featured again in the closest game of the season, against Free Foresters. Sixteen runs were still needed for the last wicket when he decided to throw caution to the wind, smacking four fours off five balls to put the matter beyond doubt. Moving to Eastbourne, Cambridge participated in yet another nail-biter against Leveson-Gower's eleven. At 92 for nought, the target of 172 seemed a formality, so the last two batsmen, one of whom was Leveson-Gower himself, decided to leave early. However, they had not reckoned with Cambridge's tenacity, and in the end the match was lost by eight runs, with numbers ten and eleven nowhere to be seen! It had been another year of unfulfilled promise, a fact brought home in crushing fashion at Lord's, where Mulholland was barred from playing because he had already been in residence for four years. Another difficult wicket meant that batting last was again a thankless task, and this time the target of 268 was just too much. Cambridge slumped to 73 all out, Naumann's brother Frank finishing the contest with a spell of four for 10. 194 runs was a sizeable victory margin, but, as the world held its breath in the summer of 1914, at least Cantabrigians could console themselves with the knowledge that the ancient series was balanced heavily in their favour – after eighty games, Cambridge had won thirty-eight, and Oxford thirty-four.

The next four-and-a-half years was effectively a period of extended hibernation for the Club, as reflected in the terse notices in the minutes. On 27 October 1914, all members of the University eleven were reported to be absent from Cambridge on military duty, and arrangements for matches were in abeyance. As a result of the lack of matches, or any other activities, subscriptions were reduced from £1 1s to 7s and 6d, and at the end of 1915, with no sign of an end to the bloodshed, the appointments of captain, secretary and assistant treasurer were indefinitely postponed. At the same time, a grant of £2 10s was awarded to the Club's loyal printer, Harry Smith, two years after his application for a benefit was declined. The only action seen at the ground during this hiatus was of the military variety, including sports like officers' races run in full uniform. But there was no pretence that everything was carrying on as normal – the daily news from France and Flanders made sure of that.

Of the 1914 side, Alban Arnold, Geoff Davies and Ken Woodroffe did not return from the war, and in all eighteen cricket Blues were added to the role of honour. Colbeck and Napier were perhaps the most notable names, but of course we will never know how many other potential Cambridge cricketers were wiped out before their time. The only bright spot was the healthy state of schools cricket, which continued unabated, and filled the pages of *Wisden* in the absence of any first-class matches. In 1919, it made A.P.F. Chapman of Uppingham one of its Public School Cricketers of the Year, following three outstanding seasons that had the cricket-loving public licking its lips in anticipation of treats in store. Here was a young player with exactly the right attributes to restore patriotic confidence when peace finally came – dashing, gentlemanly and physically beautiful. His father had been to Cambridge, as had his Uncle Charles, who played for the eleven in the 1880s without getting his Blue. What could be more natural than that young Percy should follow in their footsteps? If only the war would end, what a future awaited!

PLAYER'S CIGARETTES

A. P. F. CHAPMAN
(KENT)

Percy Chapman was one of the greatest fielders of any era.

TEN

HAPPY DAYS ARE
HERE AGAIN

In 1919 there was an air of anticipation in Cambridge quite unlike anything experienced before, but it was also mingled with some trepidation among the cricketing fraternity. As *Wisden* reported:

The Cambridge authorities approached the resumption of first-class cricket with a good deal of apprehension, no one having at the beginning of the year a remote idea as to the players who would be in residence.

Freddie Calthorpe had been offered the captaincy, but he was still serving in France when the invitation was sent. It never reached him, and since, naturally, he did not reply, John Morrison took over the job. The Varsity Match itself was doubtful when Calthorpe was being considered at the beginning of the year, but by the time Fenner's was open for nets on 24 April, the mists had cleared enough for a full fixture list to be published, with Oxford confirmed for 7 July.

The University's books filled up swiftly as the troops returned, and the students included many whose studies had been so rudely interrupted in 1914. Four old Blues, Morrison, Wood, Calthorpe and Gordon Fairbairn, were already in residence, and they were soon to be joined by John Naumann, the hero of 1913. The press was full of prospects for the forthcoming season, and particularly pressed the claims of G.M. Butler of Harrow, Gilbert Ashton of Winchester, M.D. 'Dar' Lyon of Rugby and Jack MacBryan, who had already had success with Somerset. Yet the fickle nature of sporting fate, along with the wealth of talent available, was amply demonstrated by the fact that of the four only Ashton was awarded his Blue that year. Indeed, Butler never played for Cambridge, or any other first-class team for that matter.

By early May, the weather had only permitted two or three days of practice, but the numbers attending were hugely encouraging. Cricket finally got under way again on 8 May, as Geoffrey Brooke-Taylor and Geoff Wilson opened the batting in the Freshmen's match. One new name of particular significance to emerge was that of Arthur Gilligan, already twenty-four and determined to make up for lost time. He took ten wickets in the first trial, when the *Cambridge Daily News* decided that he was merely fast-medium, but by the time of the third game, when he had another five-wicket haul against the Perambulators, the hacks had already promoted him to 'fast'. Whatever speed he bowled at, it all came the same to the opposition in the season's real curtain-raiser, which just happened to be the Australian Imperial Forces team. They rattled up 518 for seven on the first day, and declared on the second afternoon at 650 for eight. Gilligan, who bowled without any luck, took one for 130, but he escaped lightly compared with Fairbairn, whose slow leg-breaks went for 201 off just thirty-six overs. Cambridge lost comfortably by an innings, the only bright spot being a last-wicket stand of 145 between Naumann and newcomer Gerard Rotherham, mainly employed for his bowling, but living proof that there were no rabbits left in Cambridge even before myxomatosis.

The extreme depth of the batting was confirmed by the fact that six batsmen averaged 39 or more, and the compilation of another major last-wicket stand, this time an all-time Cambridge record. It came in the match against Sussex at Brighton, which turned into a comprehensive innings defeat for the southern county. Morrison got the party going with 168 in 150 minutes, and it was in full swing by the time Gilligan came in at 434 for nine. When the last dance finished sixty-five minutes later, the total had advanced by a further 177, Gilligan's contribution being a rumbustious 101 with fifteen fours and two sixes. His partner Naumann had been a little more sober, and was left on 134 not out, his only first-class hundred.

Arthur Gilligan captained England on the 1924/25 trip to Australia.

There were three other big wins to savour, but there was a feeling that the attack lacked the little bit of fire that might have brought the Light Blues even more success. Gilligan was obviously a real find, but of the rest only Gordon Fairbairn's leg-breaks looked threatening, and he was already known from before the war. Despite that, it was felt that Cambridge had a wider variety of bowlers than Oxford, and certainly there was a greater depth in batting. The biggest problem for Morrison as the Varsity Match approached was whom to leave out among such a broad spread of talent. One player he felt surplus to requirements was MacBryan, a character who seemed dogged by ill-luck in many fields. At Cheltenham he had been regarded as a future champion, but events conspired against him. As David Foot describes:

At school he had a superb cover drive. Then he put his shoulder out when playing fly-half for Bath. He was never able to hit the ball properly off the front foot through the offside again.

Having survived being a prisoner of war, he hoped for easier times ahead, but his ambitions to work in mental health were thwarted by his father, and, finally making his Test debut against South Africa in 1924, he became the only man in Test history never to bat, bowl or take a catch. His first Test, at Old Trafford, was virtually washed out and in their wisdom the selectors dropped him. He never received the invitation again. However, you could set against that the fact that he played hockey in the 1920 Olympics, and had a lifetime of sporting achievement to look back on. In truth, there is plenty of evidence to suggest that MacBryan was a curmudgeonly man with several large chips on his shoulder, a theory given sustenance by the story he recounted of how he came to be left out in 1919. Much to MacBryan's disgust, Morrison used to drink sherry out of a beer mug, something that no real gentleman would do. Our Jack made his feelings known to the skipper, who relayed them to his mother. To his great surprise, she invited MacBryan to tea, where she expressed her approval of what he had said. Despite the maternal shake of the finger, Morrison remained unmoved and could find no room for such an awkward customer in his final eleven.

When the big day finally arrived, Cambridge's lack of penetration was exposed by a patient innings from the bespectacled Miles Howell after Oxford had won the toss. He held the Light Blue attack at bay for five and a half hours for a carefully compiled 170, ensuring that Oxford couldn't lose with a total of 387. He was helped by a more exciting 70 in ninety minutes by Arthur's eldest brother Frank Gilligan, the Dark Blues' wicketkeeper. He was later to stump his brother at the end of Cambridge's first innings, and, to complete a unique double, Oxford's Frank Naumann bowled his brother John in the second innings. Wood and Conrad Johnstone got Cambridge off to a cracking start with an opening stand of 116 in 110 minutes, but only Fairbairn and Rotherham offered much resistance after that. Gilligan took six for 52 in Oxford's second innings, leaving Cambridge 276 to win. While Gilbert Ashton and Brooke-Taylor kept swinging the bat, the target was always feasible, but in the end a 45-run victory for Oxford was only fair on the run of play. More importantly, the whole occasion had been a magnificent way

Clem Gibson strengthened the attack of the great 1921 side.

to relaunch the series after a gap of five years. The crowds had flocked to watch two very worthy opponents, and once more student cricket was seen to be in rude health. It was also a great advertisement for the three-day game. The authorities experimented disastrously with a two-day County Championship in 1919, though fortunately all but one of Cambridge's games retained the longer format, with much more entertaining results. Sanity prevailed when the 1920 Championship returned to the traditional three days.

The close season saw the launch of an appeal for a memorial tablet to the war deaths in the pavilion, together with the clearing of debts incurred during the war, and the reduction of the mortgage taken out at the end of the previous century. While the square had seen no action during the war, it was still lovingly tended by Dan Hayward, Walter Watts' successor as groundsman, and the MCC, in return for an increase in its annual donation, was insistent that the Club must try to lessen its debt in peacetime. Subscriptions to the fund of five guineas or more were rewarded with life membership, and many old players dug deep, notably Lord Hawke with £10 10s and C.I. Thornton with £5.

The 1920 Freshmen's trials were again eagerly awaited, with an even greater abundance of talent on display. Chapman had come up, and he was joined by another star batsmen in Gilbert Ashton's brother Hubert. The bowling was to be considerably augmented by Clem Gibson of Eton, Norman Partridge from Malvern and, in particular, Charles 'Father' Marriott. Chapman disappointed in both matches, and was only twelfth man for the opening first-class fixture against Essex. As luck would have it, Brooke-Taylor was injured, and Chapman was able to make his debut after all. He batted as though born to the first-class arena, scoring 118 in 170 minutes of chanceless strokeplay. Hubert Ashton was almost as good in his innings of 32 and 62, and they continued in much the same vein throughout the summer. Chapman scored 613 runs at an average of nearly 41, and Ashton, helped greatly by a Herculean 236 not out against Free Foresters, 678 at 67.8. Chapman's style has never been better described than by R.C. Robertson-Glasgow:

In his Cambridge days he used no cunning, no more than Coeur de Lion would have used when knocking off some Saracen's head, and he left nothing alone. It was plain when you bowled to him that he believed himself able to score off anything, felt himself to be master of the whole armoury of the bowler's attack. ... on and just outside the off stump he had those delayed strokes that defy description, half cut and half drive, and it didn't matter how good was the length of ball.

If anything, his fielding required even more superlatives to do it justice:

At cover, in lithe and pliable youth, he was a nonpareil. Nothing stoppable seemed to escape his huge hands and telescopic reach; being left-handed, he could pounce on those balls that swerve away from cover towards third-man, and, still stooping, he would flick them back over the bails.

As for Ashton, Robertson-Glasgow couldn't seem to separate him from his brothers, merely opining that between them they possessed all known batting strokes. This was a bit harsh on Hubert for he was in fact much nearer to being a complete batsman than either of his brothers, or indeed Chapman. Digby Jephson, writing in *The Cricketer* after the 1921 Varsity Match, wrote that Ashton:

gave us a splendid exhibition of scoring strokes all round the wicket… mistakes were more than atoned for by his strokes to leg and his placing of the ball through the covers. He watches the ball as closely as, if not more closely than, any other player on either side.

It was the latter quality that made him even more dangerous, if somewhat less glamorous, than Chapman over the next three years.

That innings of Ashton's against Free Foresters was a gem, especially considering he had not gone to bed the night before: a traditional hazard of the Cambridge summer season. In four hours, he hit twenty-nine fours and a six while creating a new Cambridge record score. He also rescued the side from a perilous 178 for six in a stand of 145 with Gilligan, eventually carrying his bat in a total of 484. Marriott then took eleven wickets in the match to complete an easy victory, one of many that he was to stamp his mark on before the season was out. Born in Lancashire, and already on its books when he came down to Cambridge, Marriott later played with immense success for Kent, and would surely have appeared more than once for England if his teaching duties at Dulwich College had not interfered so much with his cricket career. In his first year at Cambridge, he was far and away the best bowler, taking fifty wickets at just over 13.5, and doing enough to finish third in the national averages overall, strangely enough behind the England opening batsmen Jack Hobbs and Wilfred Rhodes. If Hubert Ashton had few weaknesses as a batsman, there was not much that Marriott couldn't do with his leg-breaks and googlies. *Wisden* remarked approvingly: 'For a slow bowler who did so much with the ball it was remarkable how well he kept his length.' As for the rest of the attack, Gilligan, Rotherham, and the new fast bowlers Partridge and Gibson all averaged 22 or less, so Wood was never short of options if he needed to give Marriott a rest.

Such was the improvement in the attack that Cambridge arrived at Lord's having won eight and lost only two matches, and in pole position for the season's climax. Once again, Cambridge's embarrassment of riches meant that difficult decisions had to be made, including the much-criticised exclusion of Rotherham in favour of Brooke-Taylor. Crushingly for Cambridge, the rain fell solidly for the next two days and it only allowed two hours play on the third. A tactical error was perhaps made at this stage by giving over a fourth day to the match, as it may have been replayed at a later date if so much time had not already been used up. There was just enough time for Marriott to take seven wickets in a masterly spell, and for MacBryan, finally getting his Blue, to be bowled, caught and stumped off the same delivery from Reg Bettington. No wonder he bemoaned his luck in later life. Cambridge was still behind Oxford's meagre first innings total when time was called early to allow the groundstaff to prepare for the next day's Eton *v.* Harrow match. The sense of disappointment was assuaged somewhat by the selection of Chapman, Hubert Ashton and Wood for the Gentlemen against the Players, and by the knowledge that this formidable unit would retain many of its personnel for another two years.

The Freshers' matches of 1921 only served to increase the sense that the good times were just around the corner. John Bryan of Kent, who had not even been given a trial the year before, and yet another Ashton, Claude, each made a hundred, but even their achievements were dwarfed by that of the New Zealander Tom Lowry, who scored a mighty 183. Yet he had to wait his turn like everyone else, only finally getting his Blue in 1923. He did at least achieve the distinction of becoming Percy Chapman's brother-in-law when the latter married his sister Beet in 1925, and his patience was also rewarded with the New Zealand captaincy in its first ever Test match in 1929. Such was the strength of the 1921 side that he only managed four innings for Cambridge, but ironically he did have the satisfaction of taking 81 off the Light Blues' attack, playing for Somerset in the second game of the season. Unfortunately for him, any pleasure he may have felt would have been rapidly diluted by the merciless thrashing inflicted on the county by the rampant students.

The batting in that golden year was fit to rank with any from the Club's illustrious past, even if the bowling lacked some of the bite of a year before. *Wisden* was of the opinion that Cambridge 'with a little more bowling of real class would have had a first-rate team', but history can afford to be rather kinder in its verdict. Nine wins in twelve games was an exceptional effort, and it said much for the positive approach that there was only one draw. Of the two losses, one was against the mighty Australians, and the other occurred when half the team was missing due to exams. Of special note was the fielding, which 'for all-round excellence... was not surpassed by any English side' in a dismal summer for the ageing national squad. Many critics were amazed that neither Hubert Ashton nor Chapman was given a call-up, especially after Ashton became the first man of the season to score a century off the Australian attack. He had to be content with recognition by *Wisden* as one of its Cricketers of the Year, an accolade also accorded to Bryan, who scored 935 runs for Cambridge and finished sixth in the national averages after a successful long vacation with Kent. He became a very dependable county player, and went on the 1924–25 MCC tour of Australia, although he never made it into the Test side. His brief brilliance for Cambridge included an innings of 231 against Surrey in a run-feast at The Oval, and 183 against Leveson-Gower's XI. If only he had been given more than one season to show what he could do.

Thus Cambridge went to Lord's as strong favourite, but no one was quite prepared for the utter domination of the Light Blues. Digby Jephson again:

One colour, and one only, permeated the entire picture, and that colour flourishes on the banks of the river Cam. In batting, in bowling, in the art of catching and gathering the ball, and in wicket-keeping, Cambridge were yards ahead of Oxford. The captaincy of Gilbert Ashton was an object-lesson to many older and more experienced skippers of county sides. The bowling was changed with refreshing frequency, and the batsmen were never allowed to settle down... fine batting pitted against very moderate bowling... is bound to produce runs.

And so it proved. After Ashton had called correctly, Bryan opened the batting with Charles Fiddian-Green, a stylish right-hander who had made his debut for Warwickshire the previous year, and who, like MacBryan, later played hockey for England. Bryan provided a solid start with 62 before lunch, after which the crowd-pleasers Hubert Ashton and Chapman took control. Chapman went for 45, but Claude Ashton saw his brother through to another hundred, and the tail, if it could be called that, wagged in the shape of Gibson and Graham Doggart. The latter was the first in a great Cambridge dynasty, and a fine all-rounder in his own right, as well as an England footballer with a lethal left foot. A great team effort meant that Gilbert Ashton was able to declare overnight at 415 for eight, Cambridge's highest score against Oxford to that time.

Unsurprisingly, Oxford's batsmen played as if they had had the stuffing knocked out of them, despite the presence of Douglas Jardine at the top of the order. Marriott finished the match with seven wickets, and Gibson with six, as one of Cambridge's greatest line-ups finally fulfilled its destiny. There was to be a fascinating postscript to this triumphant season: at the end of August, Archie Maclaren, who had been a vociferous critic of the England set-up all summer, chose an all-amateur team to play the Australians at Scarborough. He invited five of the Cambridge side, plus old Blue Michael Falcon, to take part in a challenge that, in his opinion, would prove that the tourists could be beaten. However, his confidence seemed desperately misplaced after his eleven was ignominiously dismissed for just 43 in its first innings. Although the Australians only managed 174 in reply, the lead seemed more than enough to ensure a comfortable victory. They were not prepared for the dramatic transformation that followed, when Hubert Ashton and the South African Aubrey Faulkner put on 154 after the England XI had been 60 for four. Ashton made 75, and Faulkner 153, and Australia needed 196 to win. The excitement was incredible as the situation constantly fluctuated, but eventually Maclaren's charges came out on top by 28 runs thanks to Gibson's six for 64. There could be no more ringing endorsement of the quality of Cambridge cricket than the individual successes of this classic match, played against the toughest opposition.

After such a summer, some kind of backlash seemed inevitable, especially given the departure of some key personnel. Marriott had finished his degree, and Clem Gibson took up a business opportunity in Argentina, but the gap they left was immediately plugged by two new faces, Philip Wright of Wellingborough and the Etonian Gubby Allen. Together with Fred Browne, they managed 151 wickets in their contrasting styles, and ensured continued penetration in the attack in 1922 under Hubert Ashton's stewardship. The fact that six games were drawn was more due to

Gubby Allen was sent down before he had the chance to captain Cambridge.

the weather than anything else, and again there were only two losses, compared with five wins. Ashton was again in dominant form, compiling 852 runs at an average of 65, while Fiddian-Green stepped up a gear in the absence of Bryan, scoring 689 at 49, including hundreds in three successive matches. He was regarded by *Wisden* as 'a model of style and steadiness', something that could not be said of Browne's bowling action. He had a 'weird delivery that defies description', and indeed he was nicknamed 'Tishy' after a horse that crossed its legs at the start of a race. It was still good enough to bring him four cheap wickets in that year's Varsity Match, another one-sided affair that Cambridge led from start to finish. Patrons were granted one last chance to savour the magic of Ashton and Chapman, as they put on 172 in 135 minutes for the fifth wicket in extremely gloomy conditions. The stand is still a Cambridge record for the fixture, and Chapman's hundred was one of the classics. Allen then led the assault with nine wickets in the match, as Oxford's resistance crumbled. The drubbing handed out was even more severe than the previous year, the Dark Blues managing only 81 in their second knock after following on.

1923 saw a remarkable repetition of the Studd's feat of the 1880s, as Claude Ashton became the third successive brother to captain the side. When one considers that another brother, Percy, was only prevented from having a first-class career by the loss of an eye during the war, it becomes clear that this was truly one of the great cricketing families. Unfortunately, Claude was the least successful, as, for the first time since the war, the Club lost more matches than it won. Most of the great side of the previous two or three years had departed, and, with one notable exception, their replacements were not of the same quality. That exception was Lowry, who grasped his belated opportunity with both hands. He became the first player to score 1,000 runs in a university season, compiling four hundreds en route. Two notable wins were by nine wickets against the West Indian tourists, and seven wickets against Free Foresters, when Lowry scored 100 in eighty-five minutes as Cambridge successfully chased 375. The Varsity Match was ruined as a contest by a thunderstorm that made the wicket a minefield when Cambridge batted. In reply to Oxford's 422, Cambridge was routed for 59 and 136 by the spin twins Stevens and Bettington. Despite the weather, Cambridge could not begrudge Oxford victory, as it was by far the superior side.

Another factor in the heaviness of the defeat, the largest by an innings in the fixture's history, was the ineffectiveness of Allen, caused by an injury sustained against the MCC. It was a sad end to his Cambridge career, as he was abruptly rusticated by Trinity at the end of the summer. If he had been elected captain for 1924, he would have been admitted by another college, whatever his academic credentials. As it was, the committee chose Lowry, and Allen had to leave. He must have felt cheated of the chance to enhance a reputation that could only have been damaged by an accusation of throwing levelled against him by *Wisden*'s anonymous correspondent. It is very much at odds with other descriptions of his classical action, and certainly the press never seems to have picked up on it. Fortunately, it does not appear to have stuck, and after Cambridge he continued to make a huge contribution to the development of the game at all levels.

The new season commenced with a series of repairs and renovations to the pavilion, including staging for seats on the roof, and a new clock that was visible from the centre of the ground. The players must have wished that nobody could see them out in the middle, as they failed to win a single game at home, while losing five. Lowry spent half the season recovering from an appendix operation, but came to life on tour, thumping 133 against Northamptonshire out of a winning 322 for seven. He also led from the front against Oxford, making 68 in under an hour, to give Cambridge a first-innings lead before the close of the first day. The Harrovian Henry Enthoven pressed home the advantage the next day, scoring 104 in two and a quarter hours, although, according to *Wisden*, 'there was no distinction in his style'. Wright then polished off Oxford a second time, taking six for 49 to end his Cambridge days on a high note. A nine-wicket win was a considerable reversal of form for both parties, and brought some relief at the end of a generally miserable season.

Fortunes picked up markedly in 1925, the most exciting development being the arrival from Cheltenham of Ranji's nephew, Kumar Shri Duleepsinhji. He had raised expectations by his schoolboy feats of 1923, and now gave those with a long memory an uncanny reminder of his uncle's amazing steeliness of eye and wrist, as he compiled a brilliant 99 in the Freshers' match. The *Cambridge Daily News* was already moved to write about this new young star:

Duleepsinhji and Gilligan enjoy some mountain air.

At the moment one does not wish to say any more than that for a man of his age he has a gone a long way towards mastering the art of footwork.

The Cricketer was less able to suppress its excitement:

His batting in the Freshmen's match certainly dwarfed all else seen in the game, and it was not only the manner in which his runs were obtained that was impressive – he made them when most of his companions seemed almost helpless. Blessed with a very quick eye and having many strokes, he seems specially adept at forcing the ball to the on and late cutting. His defence, too, has improved considerably since he first obtained a place in the Cheltenham Eleven.

From the outset it was clear then that this dashing strokemaker was destined for his Blue at the first attempt, a distinction denied his famous relative in different times.

His captain, Cecil Bennett, marshalled the talents at his disposal to great effect, presiding over six wins, and only three losses. The venerable correspondent of *The Cricketer* put this upsurge in fortunes down to the unfurling of the Light Blues' flag from the top of the pavilion for the first time for many years, but more rational observers took the view that Cambridge simply had a good team. The dominant forces apart from Duleepsinhji were two old Blues, Enthoven and Rollo Meyer. Enthoven's batting won appreciative notices for its much greater appeal, while Meyer's medium-pace earned the following praise from *Wisden*:

Henry Enthoven scored Varsity Match hundreds in successive years.

A Club match from the late 1920s. R.G.H. Lowe is seated in the middle of the front row.

With his steady length, slightly varied pace and swerve, combined with speed off the pitch and some break, [he] was difficult on any wicket.

Enthoven had a monumental all-round season, scoring 775 runs and taking fifty wickets, and Meyer took fifty-five wickets at the respectable average of 20. The only element lacking from the squad was a bowler of reasonable pace, a fact exposed in the Varsity Match, when a draw became inevitable after Oxford had run up 350 and Cambridge replied with 405. At least it gave Enthoven the chance to emulate William Yardley by scoring a second century in the fixture, while Leonard Crawley, in later years a well-known golfing correspondent, came tantalisingly close to his first such landmark before falling for 98 straight after lunch. He had earlier made a crucial contribution to a staggering win against Surrey when, left to chase 426 in a day, the students had completed the task in style with no less than six wickets to spare. What made the victory even more sweet was the fact that Jack Hobbs, in the form of his life, had scored a century in each innings for Surrey.

The old cliché that sport and politics don't mix was held up for close inspection at the start of 1926, when the General Strike caused the abandonment of the opening game of the season against Middlesex – presumably the players could not be expected to make their own sandwiches! The Sussex match was also scratched due to the strike, and indeed only six of the thirteen fixtures reached a positive conclusion in a hideously wet summer. Cambridge's record was slightly flattering, as the three wins at Fenner's were against moderate opposition on soft pitches. The fourth and final win was in the game that mattered, after a tremendous tussle with

Oxford under leaden skies. A low-scoring affair was perhaps swung by a hat-trick from Richard Lowe, an England amateur football international who, before the end of Oxford's first innings, had enjoyed only a moderate cricket career:

The third ball of an over rose sharply and McBride placed it into the hands of short leg, the next, a slow yorker, sent back McCanlis; while the fifth, which kept low, touched the off stump, and knocked off a bail, bringing about the downfall of Greenstock.

Thus a vital 16-run lead was established, enough to set up a 30-run victory and to carve R.G.H. Lowe's initials in the annals of the game's most classic fixture.

Duleepsinhji began 1927 as though he meant to be the first student ever to score a thousand runs before the end of May, a purple patch exemplified by his 254 not out against Middlesex, a new Cambridge record that is likely never to be beaten. Much to the county's chagrin, he was missed in the slips on 4, but he proceeded serenely past landmark after landmark, until his innings drew to a close after four hours and thirty-four sumptuous fours. Tragically, he caught a cold in the middle of the month that developed into pneumonia and he was not strong enough to play for the rest of the summer. His health was never quite the same again, but he still managed several glorious years with Sussex and a briefly scintillating England career.

The Middlesex match was one of ten draws that year, again a reflection of lack of depth in the attack. One bonus was the form of the unnaturally tall Maurice Allom, a second year who made little impact as a Freshman. With his great height, he was able to extract a decent amount of lift at a lively pace, as he showed with an impressive display against the Army that yielded fourteen wickets for 102. He was assisted by Tom Longfield, an all-rounder in the Enthoven mould whose daughter went on to marry Ted Dexter. Not only did he take fourty-six wickets, but he also scored 504 runs at 42. Top run-scorer was the Etonian Edward Dawson, a staunch and stylish opener in his final year, who managed 951 at an average of 41. His finest hour was the hundred that brought victory against the New Zealanders, and this liking for the Kiwis' bowling was evidently in the selectors' minds when he was picked to go on the 1929–30 tour of the country. He had never made a major contribution in the Varsity Match, and 1927 was no exception, but it did not stop Cambridge registering its third win in four years. After exactly a century of competition, the Light Blues now led by forty-three games to thirty-six.

Walter Robins had shown much promise as an all-rounder at Highgate School, but had hardly been called upon to bowl in his first year at Cambridge. In 1928, his leg-breaks were revived to such an extent that he took forty-four wickets, while the New Zealander Edward Blundell, later Governor-General of his country, took forty-nine in his first season. There were still no freshers in the team, and no wins at Fenner's, an increasingly common happening. There were two real calamities, one being a thrashing by the West Indies, the other a hideous collapse against Yorkshire. At lunch on the second day, Cambridge was 15 for seven, and could only double the score before succumbing soon afterwards. Emmott Robinson took eight for 13,

Walter Robins was one of Cambridge's most entertaining all-rounders.

and the all-out total of 30 remains an unwanted record to this day. In the end the weather came to the students' rescue with their second innings teetering on 41 for five. At least the season ended with some excitement as the Varsity Match went right down to the wire. Cambridge squeaked a five-run first-innings lead, and set up a breathless finish after Robins had completed a hundred in just 105 minutes. Needing 335 to win in three hours thirty-five minutes, Oxford seemed out of it as wickets fell at regular intervals:

Nearly half an hour remained when Benson, the last man, joined Hill-Wood. For twenty minutes, amid ever-growing excitement, these two men offered a sound resistance to the Cambridge attack but, with seven minutes to go, Hill-Wood offered a chance high up close in, at short leg to Killick. The catch was missed and that mistake determined the issue of the struggle.

As soon as the 1929 season started, Tom Killick did as much as humanly possible to make up for this desperate lapse. He had already scored 823 runs before the South Africans visited Cambridge for the last game in May, and set off with the clear intent of reaching the coveted thousand by the end of the match. Alas, on 77 he dragged a long hop on to his stumps, and he was left 100 short. Nevertheless, he finished top of the Club averages, and distinguished himself by scoring two double-centuries.

The signatures of the 1929 Cambridge team, captained by Maurice Turnbull.

The first, against Glamorgan, included a century in just sixty minutes, the quickest in Cambridge's history, and also a second-wicket record stand of 290 with William Harbinson. Regrettably, this was the only game the Club looked like winning all summer, as draw after draw reflected the poverty of the attack. Glamorgan's Maurice Turnbull, captain in his final year, finally came good, beating Killick to a thousand runs, but it needed contributions from the team as a whole for talent to be turned into results.

No less than seven England players were produced in the last three years of the decade, but of those only Allom was a specialist bowler. Killick made his debut against South Africa while still an undergraduate, and four of them went on the New Zealand tour immortalised by Turnbull and Allom in their *Book of the Two Maurices*. Typifying the feeling of what might have been was Bryan Valentine, an intermittently brilliant batsman in the vein of Chapman. He went on two England tours, including the first to India, where he made a century on debut, but he never got going for Cambridge. But that was a minor concern compared with what was truly at issue. Once again, the hunt was on for a real fast bowler that could extract some life from the featherbeds of Fenner's, one who would stop county batsmen rubbing their hands with glee, if only for a few overs. Without that firepower, Cambridge could never hope to be truly competitive again.

CHURCHMAN'S CIGARETTES

M. J. TURNBULL

Turnbull was killed in action in 1944.

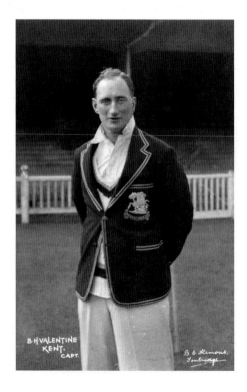

B·H·VALENTINE
KENT.
CAPT.

Bryan Valentine, an intermittently brilliant batsman.

ELEVEN

PROMISE
UNFULFILLED

The first half of the 1930s was a time of moderate achievement, but the production line of international cricketers did not slow down for an instant. The truth of the matter was that the counties no longer offered any easy matches, and the University was finding it increasingly difficult to win at home. Some of its fast bowling problems were solved straight away with the introduction of Rodney Rought-Rought from the wilds of Suffolk. His forty-three wickets cost just 18 apiece, and included a haul of seven for 36 against Middlesex that helped set up the only home win of the season. Also instrumental in this victory was Freddie Brown, fresh from the playing fields of Cambridge's Leys School, whose all-round contribution was typical of the standard he reached all season. He made nearly 700 runs at an impressive 48, and took thrity-four wickets with his combination of leg-spin and medium-pace. He was rewarded with his first England cap soon after coming down in 1931, and, of course, the captaincy itself after the war.

Another notable win was against Sussex, when the West Indian Jackie Grant made an impeccable 97. Grant had already joined the student Christian Movement, and was later a well-known evangelist, but meanwhile he was happy to show off his sporting prowess. He had played two one-day matches on the West Indies 1928 tour, and scored two goals in the Varsity soccer match that year. If Brown had to wait twenty years before captaining his country, Grant was scarcely given twenty weeks before having the mantle thrust upon him at the end of his student days. Aged just twenty-three, he was no match for the might of Bradman's Australia, but if nothing else he led by example in the field, as the Fenner's faithful knew only too well. Percy Piggott recalled a remarkable incident from the home game against Sussex that year:

Bowley snicked a ball from G.D. Kemp-Welch into the slips where it hit R.C. Rought-Rought on the wrist and glanced towards N.M.V. Rothschild, who knocked it slightly into the air. G.C. Grant, who was fielding in the gully, with that sense of anticipation which stamped

him as such a brilliant fieldsman, had meanwhile darted in the direction of the slip fields, and snatched up the catch.

Oxford must have rued the fact that it did not have Grant in its ranks, for the Varsity Match was taken out of its reach by a catalogue of errors in the field. Having gained a 26-run first-innings lead, it had every reason to be confident at the beginning of the third day:

Soon after twelve o'clock on the last day they [Cambridge] found themselves no more than 110 runs on with only four wickets to fall. Then came such a great display of batting by Killick and so many mistakes in fielding, four catches being missed off Hill-Wood, that the Light Blues added nearly two hundred runs. Even then there should have been no question of Oxford losing but their batting, after the fall of the third wicket, broke down in truly deplorable fashion.

Indeed, Oxford's last seven wickets fell for just 23, as Arthur Hazlerigg's off-spin suddenly seemed unplayable. His return of four for 17 complemented Killick's virtuoso performance – scores of 75 and 136 were a fine swansong to an accomplished academic career. His life as a vicar was sadly cut short at the age of forty-six, but at least he had the satisfaction of going out in style during a diocesan cricket match.

Opposite: *Fun and games with Percy Chapman (seated), Plum Warner (right), Freddie Brown (second left) and the actor W.B. Franklin.*

Right: *Ken Farnes, perhaps the fastest bowler ever to appear for Cambridge.*

1931 was a wretched season, alleviated only slightly by the first appearance of Ken Farnes, the fastest amateur bowler seen in England for many a year. Unfortunately, Rought-Rought couldn't reproduce the form of his first season, and wickets were even harder to come by, despite Brown's increasingly incisive performances. George Kemp-Welch, who weighed in with 1,111 runs himself, came to Lord's with a batting dilemma – should he include Rydal's Alan Ratcliffe, whose form until the final trial match had been disastrous? His 70 against Sussex in that last match gained him the twelfth man berth, but when Jack Davies fell down the hotel stairs the evening before the match, he was given a very fortunate reprieve. He did not mean to waste the opportunity.

In the first two hours of the match, he and Kemp-Welch wrested the initiative from Oxford with an opening stand of 149, before the latter fell for a brilliant 87. Although he never received prolonged support, Ratcliffe was able to pass John Marsh's long-standing record without trouble, before falling for 201 after a vigil of five hours and forty minutes. The legend has it that the Nawab of Pataudi, who had already compiled five hundreds for Oxford that year, told Ratcliffe not to expect to hold the record for long. Jim Parsons, a Rydal contemporary of Ratcliffe's and Cambridge rugby Blue, confirms its veracity:

Alan himself told me that, at the end of the day's play, Pataudi Senior came into the Cambridge dressing room, congratulated him charmingly but added, 'and tomorrow I will beat your record.'

*Alan Ratcliffe and the Nawab of
Pataudi, at Lord's in 1931.*

Ever a man of his word, the Nawab sailed past Ratcliffe's mark in only 260 minutes, finishing not out on 238 when his captain declared 68 ahead. An inexplicable collapse by Cambridge left Oxford with the simplest of tasks, but there had been plenty to keep the 30,000 paying spectators more than happy over the three days. But it was back to the drawing-board for Cambridge.

Farnes and Rought-Rought certainly bowled according to the plan in 1932, taking ninety-six wickets between them, an important factor in raising the number of wins at Fenner's to two, but totals of 34 and 81 against Nottinghamshire served to highlight a new fragility in the batting. Ratcliffe and Dulwich's Denys Wilcox scored four hundreds apiece, but support was minimal. They dominated the Varsity Match, making nearly two-thirds of Cambridge's first innings 431 between them, but the rest of the batting was so ponderous that there was never going to be enough time for a result after Oxford made a creditable 368 in reply. Farnes took five wickets, but bowled twenty-one no-balls under the old back-foot law. Rain at the end meant the game petered out, but Cambridge's lack of adventure was more to blame than any inclement weather.

John Human, a Geordie educated at Repton, provided the highlight of 1933 by scoring a century in each innings against Surrey, and completed four hundreds in all, but support was again thin on the ground in another disappointing campaign. A major surprise was the defeat of Yorkshire in a tight tussle by just 19 runs – the first win against the tykes for twelve years. Cambridge was mainly indebted to Jahangir

Khan, who took eleven wickets in the match at a brisk fast-medium. After his schooling in Lahore, Khan had made the Indian squad for the England tour of 1932, and played in his country's first ever Test. His charismatic reputation at Cambridge grew as time went on, and was augmented by feats such as throwing the stumps down from the top of the pavilion steps. Meanwhile, at the end of his first season at Cambridge, he was again thrust before the public at Lord's through his contribution to a notably controversial Varsity Match.

The controversy surrounded the use of a tactic that was virtually taboo after the tempestuous events of the previous winter – bodyline, or, to be more precise, leg theory. All three of Cambridge's premier bowlers, Farnes, Khan and Rolph Grant (brother of Jackie), employed a heavily packed leg-side field, but, according to Farnes, only his bowling could be said to be a danger to the batsman:

Their bowling relied on spin; mine with a similar field close in on the leg-side relied to a certain extent on intimidation and the difficulty of having to play rising balls on the leg stump… the infuriating thing was that many of the critics did not distinguish between this mild form of 'bodyline' and the off-spin attack that the condition of the wicket fully justified.

However, it was not intimidation of the batsmen that most pundits were concerned about. *The Times* reported:

Dull, deadly dull with never a ball that could hit the stump with never a stroke that could be attempted until the short-pitched ball came to be swept to leg for four and the barren space on the offside which on such a day should surely be busy with young men sprinting to save four runs… to relieve this dismal story which was in fact felt by everyone at Lord's, we can rejoice in the beauty of the Cambridge fielding.

Like the triumphant West Indies sides of the 1980s, the ugliness of the cricket was of no concern to the players when it produced such impressive results, and Cambridge could justifiably point to Oxford's first innings 164 as evidence. It was all to no avail though, as rain had extended the innings to the end of the second day. As it was, Oxford was still poised precariously at 79 for six in its second innings when time was called, Farnes looking particularly menacing with figures of four for 27.

If one single happening could clear a ground in the 1930s, it was the dismissal of Don Bradman. If he happened to get out for 0, then stunned silence would ensue, as though a dinner guest had just unwittingly insulted their host via a terrible faux pas. Jack Davies, in his final year at St John's, was the bowler who committed the gaffe of the year when the Australians visited Cambridge in May 1934. Frank Maskell, a teenager at the time, recalls the moment when Davies bowled the fateful ball:

I was looking over the wall at about twenty minutes to one. Fenner's was packed – they'd all come to see Bradman. He was clapped the whole way to the wicket… Jack Davies was bowling from the end where the pavilion is now… damned if he didn't clean bowl him third ball.

Ramsay Cox, photographed at home in 2004.

Davies the player will forever be remembered for this feat, but the Club is in greater debt to him for his far less ephemeral contribution as an administrator.

Despite Davies' cheeky intervention, the Australians had no problem completing an innings victory, thanks largely to a double-century by Bill Ponsford. The end was delayed by some lusty blows by Ramsay Cox, who made a not out 50 batting at number ten. Cox was a sprightly nonagenarian at the time of writing, one of Cambridge's oldest surviving players. Sadly, although twelfth man at Lord's, he never received his Blue. His memory of Harold Larwood was crystal clear, which is probably more than can be said of Larwood's recall of the following incident:

I played for Cambridge against Nottinghamshire in 1934. Harold Larwood played for Notts as a batsman. After play one day we were having a drink in the bar, which was run by Dan Hayward. He had some local port, which Harold partook of rather much. The result was that Bill Voce and myself had to take him back to the Castle Hotel and put him to bed!

The Cambridge batsmen scored fifteen hundreds that year, and had a lot to do with the fact that the Light Blues received only three beatings, as opposed to six the previous year. Both Human and Roger Winlaw hit five centuries, and between them they managed over 2,000 runs, including a Cambridge record fourth-wicket stand of 275 against Essex. Another record was created against Oxford, when Tony Allen and Grahame Parker put on 205 for the first wicket. Regrettably, Oxford had begun the match with the little matter of 415, and although Cambridge got to within 15, too much time had already been taken up for there to be a positive result. To cap it all, 'only' 24,000 attended the match because it clashed with the Old Trafford Test!

Parker was rewarded for his form in the Varsity Match with the captaincy for 1935. A good enough rugby player to play full-back for England, he also proved an inspirational leader. The Club won five games for the first time for a decade, recovering from a dismal start of three heavy defeats in a row at Fenner's. Even so, Cambridge was not fancied coming into the big match, despite a morale-boosting win in the last warm-up match against Sussex. The team's chances were boosted in a novel manner on the second evening, as described by Freshman Norman Yardley:

Sir Harry Preston... a connoisseur of champagne... always insisted that a visiting team staying at the 'Royal Albion' should drink some of special vintage with him... so magnums of champagne were brought into the lounge there and then... I never remember drinks so sparkling and delightful... after that champagne the first ball of the morning flashed down at such a pace that Greenwood, who was 70-odd not out, never saw it... in thirty-five minutes the game was over and we had won.

Something similar must have been on tap for the Varsity Match, which Cambridge controlled after an uncertain start. Parker played a captain's knock of 76 not out after winning the toss, and then the Jamaican Jock 'Monkey' Cameron took seven for 73

Norman Yardley and Paul Gibb, mainstays of the batting in the 1930s.

with his leg-breaks, reminding the cognoscenti of his ten wickets in an innings at Lord's as a Taunton schoolboy. Oxford was left a target of 305 in five hours and forty minutes, well within the compass of a strong batting line-up. However, Jahangir and Rydal's Wilf Wooller broke the back of the innings, and thereafter the Dark Blues never looked like winning. It was just reward for one of Cambridge's best captains, who had managed to mould a team that was far more than the sum of its parts, and would remain so for at least another year.

Khan and Wooller enhanced their burgeoning reputations at the start of the 1936 season when they dismissed Warwickshire for just 43, Khan taking six for 11 on a batsman's wicket. Wooller took seven for 20 in the second innings for good measure, setting up a win by 287 runs. This performance gave the students a momentum that they sustained for the rest of the season, despite the abysmal weather. A further win followed against the Army, and a long sequence of draws was only interrupted by a loss to Essex in a closely fought encounter. One of the tamest of the draws was the MCC match at Lord's, but it was at least enlivened by a uniquely bizarre occurrence, again described by Norman Yardley:

Jahangir Khan was bowling, Tom Pearce batting, the bowler ran up and delivered the ball, the batsman shaped to play a shot – but there was no sound of the ball hitting the bat, yet the ball dropped in the blockhole! I ran in from slip to see what had happened, and as two or three of us gathered round we found a dead sparrow there beside the ball. The bird had evidently chosen that inauspicious moment to fly across the pitch very low, the ball had hit it, and murder had been done 'out on the middle' before the eyes of thousands of unwitting spectators. What a theme for a thriller!

The sparrow killed by Jahangir Khan in 1936, now in the Memorial Gallery at Lord's.

The bird was quickly stuffed and put on display in the Long Room, assured of an immortality not granted to many of its avian friends.

Cambridge was still not fancied for the Varsity Match, despite all evidence to the contrary, but captain Hugh Bartlett certainly increased his team's chances by winning the toss. His batsmen did not let him down, running up 432, a new Cambridge record for the fixture. Everybody scored runs apart from Bartlett himself, a grave disappointment to the many fans of his elegant left-handed batting, which had yielded five centuries during his student career. Jahangir Khan finished his time at Cambridge on a much higher note, taking six wickets to go with his 49 runs, but it was new leg-spinner John Brocklebank of Eton that had Oxford bamboozled. A nephew of Stanley Jackson, he flighted the ball well at above-average pace, and was too much for any but the fleetest-footed of batsmen in this match, snaring ten in all. The Dark Blues followed on over 200 behind, and only just managed to drag the match into a fourth innings. Another easy triumph for Cambridge left the critics confounded once again. Wooller retired from Cambridge life a happy man, doubly so as he had only just escaped being stripped of his degree. Caught by the police after a night of student pranks that included the removal of a public telephone from its box, he managed to stall the legal process just long enough to avoid going to court during term, and was merely barred from the May Ball and fined £5. Those were the days!

During the close season, the Club made a momentous and felicitous decision, one that would be of profound benefit to young cricketers for decades to come. The minutes of the Annual General Meeting on 29 October reveal all:

The dashing Hugh Bartlett.

The question of the appointment of a new custodian in succession to D.M. Hayward, who retired at the end of September, was considered. It was resolved to recommend to the CUCC and Athletic Club Ltd. Executive committee that Cyril Coote, at present assistant groundsman to Trinity Hall Amalgamated Clubs, be appointed.

Never can such a bland statement have borne such glad tidings, for Coote turned out to be far more than just an excellent groundsman. Many of those who came under his wing have spoken of his supreme coaching and mentoring skills, and of a character that could never be replaced once he had gone. Fortunately his reign was a long one.

Meanwhile, however, the Club's on-field fortunes were temporarily on the wane. Although there were three wins in 1937, these had to be set against seven losses, including a convincing one against Oxford, despite a fine hundred by Yardley. He was also instrumental in winning the closest game of the season, against Hampshire. Having already taken nine wickets in the match, he came to the rescue at the crucial time, with Cambridge floundering at 35 for six in pursuit of 142 to win. His innings of 64 saw the Blues home for the loss of only one more wicket, and salvaged something from a disappointing season. One problem was the old chestnut of assembling a fully representative side. Fourteen public school captains were in residence, and yet not one of them played in the Varsity Match. As Yardley bemoaned:

I cannot help deploring the fact that… where amateur cricket reaches, in general, its highest point, it is so difficult to produce teams that are truly representative or that win the victories they ought. Even if the best cricketers can be got together there are peculiar difficulties, at any university, in welding them into an effective team.

A very modern problem indeed, and one that Yardley himself would have the pleasure of trying to solve, as he was elected captain for 1938.

Leading England against the might of Don Bradman's all-conquering 1948 Australians must have seemed a picnic compared with trying to kick-start Cambridge that year. The cupboard was finally bare, and the only bright spot was the form of Paul Gibb, who scored over a thousand runs, including a century against Oxford, while keeping wicket very proficiently. There had been some controversy when he replaced Billy Griffith behind the stumps, but, in another modern bit of thinking, the selectors had opted for the better batsman. Such was Gibb's form that he was called up for the Old Trafford Test, but his debut was delayed by Manchester's over-moist climate; the match was abandoned without a ball bowled. When he did finally play, against South Africa during that winter, he made a hundred in his first match, a feat emulated by Griffith when he was finally called up on the 1947–48 tour of the West Indies.

The last two seasons before the Second World War produced eleven losses but not a single victory. Indicative of this nadir in the team's fortunes was the creation of a new record for Fenner's, 636 runs in a single day by the Free Foresters. George

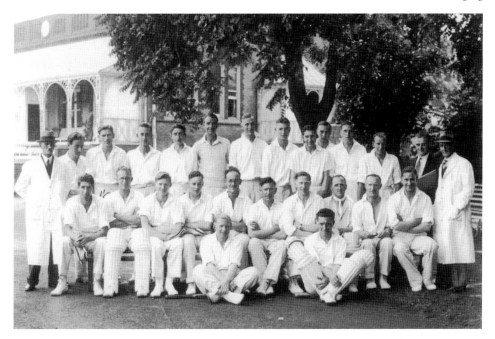

An alternative Varsity Match – the college servants teams at Fenner's in 1937.

Mann, another future England captain, and John Thompson of Tonbridge created their own little bit of history in 1939, compiling a new record opening stand for Cambridge of 262 against Leicestershire, but in the end it was only the platform for a dull draw. At least the last pre-war Varsity Match brought out some fighting spirit when the Light Blues were set an unlikely 430 to win in five hours. At 155 for five there seemed no hope, but now Patrick Dickinson, an all-rounder of hitherto negligible achievement, scored a remarkable hundred, backed up by number eleven Jack Webster, who scored an equally unlikely 60. The margin of defeat was only 45 in the end, and the never-say-die attitude displayed that day was exactly what was required in the more testing conflict that cast a shadow over everything else for the next six years.

TWELVE

RUNS GALORE

The authorities learnt their lesson from the First World War that abandoning sport altogether was not the way to improve morale, and so cricket continued at Cambridge and other places of learning, albeit against less testing opposition. The playing programme for 1940 was very much truncated, with just two three-day matches. The first, against a British Empire eleven, proved to be a walkover, as Cambridge strolled to 518 before declaring and bundling the visitors out twice in quick succession. John Thompson, now captain, and Jack Webster, the opening bowler, remained from the 1939 team, and they were joined by two impressive new recruits in Eric Conradi of Oundle and John Bridger of Rugby. Starting with the Freshers' Match, Conradi scored centuries in the only three games he played, and later returned to academia to claim his Blue in the first post-war season, although by then his form had deserted him. Bridger batted elegantly for Hampshire after the war, but his appearances were inevitably restricted by his scholastic career. Webster took six for 48 in the other match played, against a Universities eleven, which was the closest thing to a Varsity Match. Fenner's was mooted as the venue for the Oxford game, but nothing ever came of it, and thoughts turned back to Lord's for future wartime encounters.

1941 set the pattern for the rest of the war, in which a one-day Varsity Match at the end of June was preceded by an extensive series of shortened warm-up games. Cambridge had the distinct advantage of being able to play a full season at home, while Oxford was condemned to wander after The Parks was commandeered for the war effort. The Light Blues easily won four of the five games, and came agonisingly close to making a clean sweep of it in 1943. Set 290 to win, Oxford was hanging on grimly at 202 for nine when stumps were drawn. Even more exciting was the finish in 1942, when Oxford lost four wickets in ten minutes, including the captain, last man out off the seventh ball of the last over, as the clock struck seven (the country was on double summer time, and the 1939 experiment with eight-ball overs continued through the war).

The 1944 Varsity Match. Barling of Oxford is bowled by Dunkerley.

These Varsity Matches, although attended almost as well as ever, are not counted in the official series, partly due to their length, and partly due to the extraordinary conditions cricketers found themselves playing in. Life in Cambridge was incredibly busy, with most students only attending for two or three terms, and having to take part in cadet training twice a week along with their normal activities. Cricket most definitely took a back seat. In these circumstances, it was felt that a Blue could not be awarded, but Cambridge did at least award colours, consisting of a light blue cap with dark blue stripes. If this was an attempt to create an appearance of normality at cricket's headquarters, elsewhere there were plenty of rude reminders of reality. Malcolm White, wicketkeeper and Club secretary in 1944, recalls:

I was staying in the Russell Hotel, Russell Square, in London, on the night before the University Match on 24th June when I was woken up by a tremendous bang in the Square outside. This was caused by a so-called flying bomb fired at us by the German forces. Luckily no-one was hurt but there was a fair amount of damage which included broken windows in my bedroom!

Taking on Oxford must have seemed like a cakewalk after a night like that.

As for Fenner's, just for a change there was something of a financial crisis, despite cricket continuing through the war. Yet another appeal was launched, and this became even more urgent when two bombs were dropped on the ground in October 1940. The first fell near one of the tennis courts, shattering much of the pavilion's glass in the process, while the second crashed against the high boundary wall, demolishing nearly 100 feet of brickwork. It was particularly fitting that the pavilion was repaired after the war through a large donation by Lady Diana Kemp-Welch, widow of the 1931 captain, who had been killed during an air raid in London in June 1944. Particular mention must also be made of Claude Ashton and Roger Winlaw, lost in the same flying accident, Ken Farnes, also killed in the air, and Maurice Turnbull, who fell in action in Normandy. Although the roll-call was smaller than in the First World War, the waste was no less great.

On 4 May 1946, Hugh Griffiths bowled the first ball of the season to Cyril Washbrook, and first-class cricket at Fenner's began again in earnest after a gap of seven years. Although many of the squad, including those returning to Cambridge after their wartime taster courses, were more mature than most undergraduates, time had stood still as far as the team's performances were concerned. Griffiths, later a High Court Judge and president of Glamorgan, took six wickets in that first innings against Lancashire, and five against Oxford, but he received precious little support. Only Guy Willatt, later a popular captain of Derbyshire, showed any consistent form with the bat, scoring 111 against the MCC in the season's only success. There were six defeats in nine games, four of them by an innings, and it was no surprise that the side was given little chance in the annual clash at Lord's. As it turned out, this was

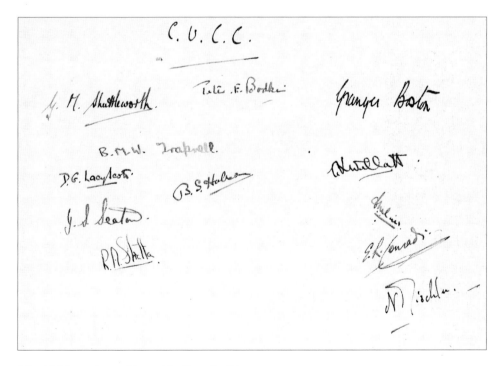

The 1946 squad was skippered by Peter Bodkin.

a fair assessment, but it was only a brilliant knock of 142 in just under three hours by Martin Donnelly that really highlighted the gap between the old rivals, fairly reflected in the victory margin of seven wickets.

Donnelly was at it again a year later, scoring 81 to back up a record second-wicket stand of 226 between Keighley and Pawson after Oxford won the toss and batted. This time Cambridge managed to bat out time, thanks largely to Willatt and two promising newcomers in Trevor Bailey of Dulwich, and Doug Insole, later the first grammar school boy ever to lead the Light Blues. Bailey added considerable bite to the attack, and with Griffiths was the main reason for a significant improvement in the playing record. There may have been only two wins, but only three games were lost, with eight draws in a rather wet summer. Hardly cause for celebration, but an improvement none the less, and, just as importantly, the crowds had returned in force, especially for the visit of the South Africans and the Varsity Match; for the second year running, more than 20,000 had flocked to St John's Wood to see the ancient foes in combat. But how long could such enthusiasm last?

The 1948 side was considerably bolstered by the return of John Dewes, who in 1945 had impressed the selectors so much by scoring 1,000 runs before the end of May that he was picked for the third Victory 'Test' at the age of eighteen. His initial first-class innings for Cambridge could not have been more inauspicious, as he was caught off Ken Cranston for a duck. The score was soon 65 for four, with Bailey

Trevor Bailey in the nets.

The South Africans at Fenner's in 1947.

already establishing his reputation as a 'barnacle' by scoring 3 in half an hour. At this point, Insole came to the rescue, along with another debutant, Hubert Doggart, son of Graham from the side of the early 1920s. Once Insole had gone for 66, Doggart played more freely, scoring a second hundred in only 110 minutes, and finishing on 215 unbeaten when the innings closed at 386. Rain confined the game to that one innings, but it had held off long enough for Doggart to become the first player in England since Tom Marsden in 1826 to score 200 on first-class debut. Doggart himself recalls:

Wisden *records that providence was kind to me that day. I can certainly recapture the pleasure of hitting Dick Pollard's slower ball through the covers; the satisfaction of the leg tickle… that brought me what Brian Johnston likes to call 'the coveted three figures'; and the delights of Glynis Johns as a mermaid in* Miranda *at the cinema in Regent Street, in the mellow evening of a memorable day.*

The *Daily News'* columnist 'Looker-On' recorded the opinion of one old pavilion sage that he was already 'a better bat than his father', something that could probably not be said of his son Simon, who was awarded his Blue four times in the 1980s. At least the latter had the pleasure of completing the line from grandfather to grandson, making the Doggarts only the second family after the Lytteltons to have three successive generations playing cricket for Cambridge.

The scorebook entry for Doggart's first first-class innings.

The Club suddenly had two new stars in the making. Insole, himself pressed into keeping wicket that year in the absence of an outstanding alternative, spent long enough batting at the other end to be able to give a clear description of their contrasting styles:

John Dewes was a very solid, generally unadventurous, left-handed opener. He played quick bowling well, with little or no apprehension. He was a good cutter, and strong off his legs. Hubert Doggart was elegant, even flamboyant. Very good through the covers. Quite a quick scorer. Good judge of a run. Mostly a forward player.

Dewes was considered good enough to be picked for the last Test against Australia, while Doggart made his debut against the West Indies in 1950. Meanwhile, there were plenty of runs to be made for Cambridge, peaking in 1949 when they both made over 1,200. There efforts were to no avail in 1948, when a poor season was crowned by an ignominious innings defeat in the Varsity Match. Doug Insole recalls one of the factors that exacerbated the gulf between the two sides:

'Tonker' Urquhart, so named because he never hit the ball off the square… had a remarkable Varsity Match. A useful medium-paced seam bowler, he just made the side ahead of a rival claimant. We batted for the whole of the first day, and he was run out for 0. He twisted his ankle in the nets on the morning of the second day and was unable to take any further part in the match, to the chagrin of his great rival, who fielded substitute throughout!

1949 started equally unfavourably, with a heavy defeat against Sussex, although Dewes' absence was a contributory factor. His first outing of the season was against Essex, now including his old friend Trevor Bailey. Bailey took the new ball after Insole had won the toss, and his partner Peter Smith soon bowled Robert Morris for 8, bringing Doggart in earlier than he had hoped. He was soon into his stride, however, as the total reached 121 for one at lunch. After the interval, the friendly rivalry between the pair continued, as they vied with each other to score the first Cambridge 100 of the season. Doggart won the race, reaching his in two hours twenty minutes. Dewes' was missed, off a caught and bowled at 98, but he was not far behind, completing the landmark in 165 minutes.

The crowd willed the pair on to even greater heights after tea, as the records started to tumble. The first to fall was the Cambridge second-wicket record of 331, set in 1929 by Harbinson and Killick against Glamorgan. Then, just after the 400 came up, they overtook the English record 398 of William Gunn and Arthur Shrewsbury made back in 1890. With stumps being drawn at 441 for one, the question was could they beat the world record of 455 set only the previous winter by K.V. Bhandakar and B.B. Nimbalkar? So far they had put on 429 in five hours ten minutes, Doggart hitting a five (he seemed to specialise in these) and twenty-five fours, and Dewes twenty-one boundaries.

Dewes and Doggart leave the field at the end of their epic stand against Essex in 1949.

Word had certainly got about on the Monday morning, as the crowd had swollen to over 1,000, and the media were present en masse. Unfortunately for them, the protagonists remembered that they were trying to win a game of cricket, and Insole made the unpopular but reasonable decision to declare overnight. The sensation seekers dwindled away, pondering what might have been. It had clearly been a joint decision; Insole explained to the press 'I asked the two batsmen whether they wanted to go on, and they said "no".' They would have to be content with the new English record, which they held until 1974, when John Jameson and Rohan Kanhai marched past it.

One journalist at least had been forewarned by Insole:

On the Saturday evening I met E. W. Swanton in Cambridge, and told him that I had declared, so that his Monday column announced the fact, but the Press as a whole did not know... a newsreel car with a camera on its roof was waiting on the cinder track which surrounds the ground, and immediately I arrived the cameraman asked my advice as to the best place to film the momentous event. When I explained that I had declared he grinned tolerantly... when he saw that I meant it, he said: 'It's a national tragedy' and drove out of the ground.

National tragedy or not, Insole still believes he made the right decision in the broader interests of the game:

THE UNIVERSITY 1st Inns		2nd Inns
1. J. G. Dewes not out 204		*J. G. Dewes*
2. R. J. Morris b Smith 8		
3. G. H. G. Doggart not out 219		*Hubert Doggart*
4. J. H. H. Anton		
5.*D. J. Insole		
6. A. C. Burnett		
7. M. H. Stevenson		
8.†O. B. Popplewell		
9. P. J. Hall...............................		
10. B. J. K. Pryer..........................		
11. P. A. Kelland		
Extras...... 10		Extras...... ...
Total (1 wkt decl.)...... 441		Total............... ...

```
 1  2  3  4  5  6  7  8  9  10    1  2  3  4  5  6  7  8  9  10
12 ... ... ... ... ... ... ... ... ...  ... ... ... ... ... ... ... ... ... ...
```

ESSEX 1st Inns		2nd Inns
1. Dodds T. C.		
2. G. H. West		
3. Cray S. J.................................		
4. Vigar F. H.		
5. Morris W. B.		
6. T. E. Bailey.............................		
7.*T. N. Pearce		
8. Smith R.		
9. Dines W. J.		
10.†Taylor B.		
11. Price E. J.		
Extras...... ...		Extras...... ...
Total............. ...		Total............... ...

```
 1  2  3  4  5  6  7  8  9  10    1  2  3  4  5  6  7  8  9  10
... ... ... ... ... ... ... ... ...  ... ... ... ... ... ... ... ... ... ...
```

* Captain   † Wicket-keeper   Umpires: H. Palmer & F. S. Lee

An up-to-date card will be produced at commencement of day and after lunch and tea, but wickets will be added at other times when possible.

Price 3d.   **May 11, 12 & 13 : v. Yorkshire**

The scorecard at the end of the partnership, signed by the participants.

I can see no reason, in a three-day game, for batting on into the second day unless the wicket is deteriorating and there are real hopes of bowling the opposition out twice. In trying to put together a team, I didn't want to get involved in a boring draw because I wanted to see my players in varied circumstances – like chasing runs and bowling economically to prevent the other side winning.

Even though a draw in this match meant Insole's enterprise went unrewarded, the fact that Dewes and Doggart didn't get to break the record gave them their own curious kind of immortality, and they remain Cambridge's equivalent of the 'Middlesex twins', Edrich and Compton. They also had a significant influence over the fate of that year's Varsity Match, a surprise Light Blue triumph by seven wickets after Oxford had left a target of 133 in ninety-five minutes. Cambridge had batted solidly all the way down in the first innings, and then the impressive new ball pairing of John Warr and O.J. Wait did enough damage to force Oxford to follow on. Warr had been 'discovered' in the pre-season nets after coming from Ealing with a minor reputation as a batsman, and was soon opening the bowling on a regular basis. Such was his progress that he was selected to tour Australia with the MCC in 1950, although his performances there confirmed that he was just short of international class.

May of 1950 was the coldest for many a year, the average temperature in Cambridge being five degrees lower than normal, but Cyril Coote was determined that he would still produce a blameless wicket for the visit of the West Indians in the middle of the month. As it turned out, it was if anything too easy-paced, with both sides gorging themselves in an unprecedented run feast. Hubert Doggart, elected captain ahead of Dewes, had no hesitation in taking advantage of the batsman-friendly conditions, and watched contentedly as his old sparring partner and freshman David Sheppard built a huge first-innings stand. They were finally parted at 343, but Sheppard carried on until tiredness finally took its toll when he had made 227. Ignoring the precedent set by Insole, Doggart batted on the next day, declaring the next morning at 594 for four. Anything the students could do, the West Indies could do even better, as the records continued to fall. The game was left drawn with the tourists 730 for three, the highest score ever made against Cambridge, as was Everton Weekes' 304 not out. Finally, the number of runs per wicket in the match, 189, is comfortably a world record.

Happily, not every game at Fenner's that year was so gloriously futile, as the Club registered wins against Leicestershire and the Free Foresters. Dewes and Sheppard remained in epic form, scoring nine hundreds between them, and going one better than against the West Indies with a first-wicket stand of 349 against Sussex, a Cambridge record that will surely remain unbeaten for a long time to come. Another to make an impact was one Peter May of Charterhouse, rated by most as the best home-grown Light Blue since the Second World War. He was not as prolific as the openers this year, but he did have the satisfaction of scoring 227 not out against Hampshire. All the brilliant batting on display during the season counted for nothing when it came to the unbearably tense atmosphere of the Varsity Match, and only Sheppard held his nerve with 93 in a disappointing first-innings effort. Oxford's reply was even worse, and Cambridge would probably have won if rain had not washed out the majority of the first day's play. As it was, Cambridge played safe when setting Oxford an impossible target, a reflection of the importance still given to this one-off match by participants and audience alike. Only when crowds started to dwindle in later years did a more carefree attitude come to be adopted.

1951 was an especially wet summer at Fenner's, but it didn't stop it being another classic year for University batsmanship. Peter May topped the first-class averages, with Sheppard not far behind, and the bowlers were particularly happy, with Warr, Wait and the Harrovian off-spinner Robin Marlar all taking over forty wickets for Cambridge. Despite this, there were no home wins, but three good victories on tour, and a narrow defeat by Oxford after a dour struggle. May's improvement was rewarded by his first England cap against South Africa, which he marked with a fine hundred, as he did the game against Middlesex, the most exciting seen at Fenner's for many a year. Sheppard went one better by scoring two separate hundreds in the match, enabling him to set the county a target of 321 in 200 minutes. At the start of the last over, 8 runs were needed with two wickets left. Marlar took a wicket with the first ball, and somehow the batsmen scrambled seven runs off the next four. The scores remained level when no runs were scored off the last ball, and the closest draw in Cambridge's long history was the result.

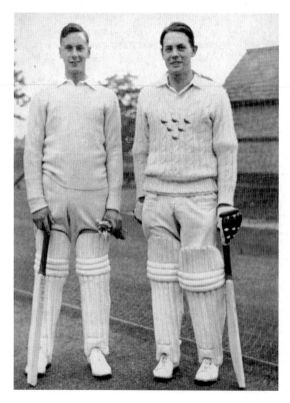

Young Sheppard and May before their first game for Cambridge.

Sheppard was at it again in 1952, creating at least four new batting records as well as captaining with great gusto. He scored 1,581 runs at an average of 79, with seven hundreds, both the aggregate and the number of three-figure scores being all-time records for either of the great seats of learning. Furthermore, he closed his stellar student career with a total of 3,545 runs and fourteen hundreds. The aggregate was later beaten by Mike Brearley, who had twice as many innings, and no one else has scored more than nine hundreds for either university. Yet it is May that remains in the public consciousness as the great post-war amateur batsman, perhaps because Sheppard never had enough time to devote to cricket once the call of the cloth became too great.

The young preacher shows how to keep a straight bat.

The latter was also instrumental in the only victory against a county, after Cambridge had got off to a wretched start. Not only were the Light Blues 110 behind after their first innings against Worcester, but Cuan McCarthy, their new fast bowling sensation from South Africa, was called for throwing for the only time in his career. He had toured England with the Springboks the previous year with no problems, but now he was leading the attack murmurs had begun to grow about the legality of his action. A mild-mannered man, he retired from the game soon after on the basis that he didn't want to bowl if it was thought his action was unfair. Meanwhile, helped by the dogged Raman Subba Row of Whitgift, Sheppard hit a personal best 239 not out to pilot Cambridge to an impressive six-wicket win against the clock, and the odds.

The Varsity Match, Sheppard's last, saw him in tandem with Subba Row again after Cambridge had got off to a stuttering start in reply to Oxford's painfully slow 272. Sheppard reached 127 and Subba Row 94, before Marlar's breezy 48 not out enabled a declaration that left a superior attack four hours to bowl the Dark Blues out a second time. McCarthy made early inroads, but the Australian Alan Dowding made a vital fifty to lead a desperate rearguard action. Fast bowler Alan Coxon resisted stubbornly to the end, despite a ferocious assault from McCarthy. Sheppard recalls what happened after one particularly vicious short ball:

Raman Subba Row bowls to Manjrekar in 1952. Sheppard and May are in the action again. Cuan McCarthy is at first slip.

Robin Marlar canvassing in his attempt to become an MP in the 1960s.

Most cricketers would have guessed that the next ball might be very fast and short. It was, but Coxon had decided to rush up the wicket before he bowled. The ball struck him on the forehead: it was not a glancing blow, for the ball fell beside him. We all rushed forward to see if he was all right, expecting him to collapse at any moment. But he nodded his head briskly, and went back to the wicket.

Coxon, and Oxford, lived to fight another day.

There were many instances of Robin Marlar's positive and idiosyncratic captaincy in 1953, as recalled by Richard Turner, twelfth man at Lord's that year. After beating Middlesex at home, the scholars went on their traditional tour:

At Old Trafford a Lancashire batsman skied a ball between three off-side fielders, each of whom could have caught it with ease. Robin yelled out 'Keith!', but Keith wasn't playing that day...

Moving to Folkestone, Kent, needing 251 to win, were 60 without loss when Turner dropped a simple chance on the boundary. Marlar's fury prompted him to take three wickets in five balls and eight for 32 in all as Cambridge won by 134 runs. With a victory against MCC into the bargain, the omens were good for a second post-war Varsity Match win, especially if Marlar could keep up the form that had already earned him forty-nine wickets during the summer.

Oxford's Birrell is caught by Gerry Alexander at the start of the 1953 Varsity Match.

This was still a boom time for the great Lord's social occasions, and *Wisden* refers apologetically to a crowd of 'only' 8,000 on the first day, as the game clashed with the rival attraction of champions Surrey against Yorkshire at The Oval. The first day belonged to Colin Cowdrey, who gave a 'delightful' exhibition in compiling 116 before becoming one of Marlar's five victims. Future West Indies wicketkeeper Gerry Alexander, 'discovered' the previous year at Fenner's, jarred the middle finger of his right hand, exacerbating an injury picked up earlier in the season, and fellow Jamaican Vincent Lumsden had to take over behind the stumps.

In reply to Oxford's 312, Cambridge batted with a 'lack of resolution' apart from Alexander, who stayed for an hour and a half despite his injury. Oxford had a lead of 121, and hoped to bat Cambridge out of the game. However, Marlar continued where he had left off in the first innings, taking three wickets for 11 in a spell of forty-nine balls. The third was the vital one of Cowdrey, caught one-handed by Alexander, back behind the timbers. Before the close, the pendulum swung back towards Oxford, as South African Fellows-Smith indulged in some lusty hitting, leaving his side on 111 for five at the end of the second day. Once again, as the twelfth man remembers, the captain was spurred on by an external annoyance:

On the final morning of the Varsity Match Robin, in his bath, read some scathing comments by Jim Swanton about his dilatory progress to the wicket the previous day. Oxford must have regretted that he read The Daily Telegraph.

Dennis Silk, hero of the 1953 Varsity Match.

Indeed they must. A lead of 232 was a useful platform for a final assault, but Marlar continued to flight the ball superbly, and the crease-bound Oxford capitulated in only half an hour on the last morning, losing the last five wickets for just 15. Marlar had taken twelve wickets in the match for only 143. Cambridge had been given a good chance, needing 238 in 320 minutes. Dennis Silk, later headmaster of Radley School, soon became very conscious that it was all down to him, as he lost partners at regular intervals. He was forced to concentrate on defence, and at the fall of the eighth wicket, 46 were still needed with only thirty-five minutes left. Marlar attracted some slow handclapping as he appeared to be playing for the draw, but Silk suddenly seized the initiative, hitting Allen for three powerful drives to the boundary. With five minutes, a maximum of two overs, left, Silk cut Allen for four, and off the fifth ball a neat deflection to square leg was enough to see Cambridge home. For those who had been at Fenner's to watch Middlesex in 1951, the excitement was almost too much.

Some, including the skipper, see 1953 as a watershed, in the sense that from this time the deep well of talent seemed to be gradually drying up. Certainly, *Wisden* thought there weren't any class players in 1954, although that is a little harsh on the Sri Lankan Gamini Goonesena, who had already played as a professional for Nottinghamshire, and took fifty-seven wickets in his first year with Cambridge. Jack Pretlove scored four hundreds, exhibiting 'a brilliantly crisp almost square cut', and he followed this up in 1955 with another century in the drawn Varsity Match, which Cambridge had much the better of, a reversal of the previous year, when

Cambridge couldn't quite press home its advantage in 1955.

Mike Smith's double-hundred left the Light Blues hanging on grimly at the end. In his second season, Goonesena topped both batting and bowling averages, and completed a match double in a resounding victory against Warwickshire. He was sorely missed during 1956, after suffering a suspected punctured lung, and was only just back in time for the Varsity Match, another close finish ending in a draw after a defiant last innings display by Oxford. Cambridge had notched up seven wins in all over these three campaigns, but only one was at Fenner's, where wickets were always harder to come by.

1957 started just as disappointingly, with no victories again at Fenner's, but at least the faithful were rewarded with the coming of age of Ted Dexter as a batsman. He had made a good impression as a fresher the year before, even if his results had been unspectacular. Indeed, as 'Lord Ted' confessed:

Cricket still remained a lighthearted sideshow in the overall scheme of the Dexter lifestyle, to the extent that an agreed appearance for Sussex later in the year was forsaken for the delights of Copenhagen and an irresistible young lady called Lisa. If her tough old uncle had not insisted on early morning swims in the North Sea, I might never have come back.

To everyone's relief, he did come back, and not long after became engaged to Susan Longfield, daughter of the 1927/28 Blue. Meanwhile, back in Blighty, now firmly committed to cricket ahead of golf, he tightened up his technique under the watchful eye of Cyril Coote, with spectacular results:

I made a hundred before lunch against Lancashire and finished with 185. True, Statham and Tattersall were rested that game but... there were certainly no scrubbers in that Lancashire side... I quickly realized that the wicket was good and I was feeling so confident that only my own carelessness would get me out. We are back again with the vital importance of the good wicket for the budding batsman. On a bad wicket against those bowlers I might well have been out in my second over, dispirited and having learned nothing.

Dexter found himself at the helm for the return match in Liverpool, a game that seemed to be following a familiar pattern when Cambridge was 209 for eight on the first day. Two and a half hours later, the scoreboard showed a miraculous transformation after Geoff Cook and fast bowler Colin Smith, himself already on Lancashire's books, had created a new record ninth-wicket stand of 200. Then Bob Barber, later an England opening batsman, exploited a turning pitch to great effect, taking seven wickets with his leg-breaks, and leading Cambridge to a convincing innings win.

A further win on tour against Gloucestershire set up the Light Blues nicely for the annual trip to St John's Wood, but nobody was prepared for what followed. Faced with a cloudy day and a green pitch, Oxford still batted first, but was made to regret its folly by lunchtime, when it was reeling at 48 for eight. Ossie Wheatley, of King Edward's School, Birmingham, bowling with 'accuracy and liveliness... allied with the ability to make the ball move sufficiently off the pitch to worry uncertain batsmen', took three for 4 in seven overs at the start, and finished with five for 15 as Oxford struggled to 92 all out after the interval. Cambridge found the going only

Ted Dexter bowls Yorkshire's Frank Lowson in 1958.

slightly easier in reply, reaching the close at 108 for five. Next day the sixth wicket fell at 135, and Goonesena was joined by Cook. Once again, the latter was involved in a thrilling rescue act, as the seventh wicket put on 289 in just three-and-three-quarter hours before Goonesena fell for 211. His first hundred had taken four hours in taxing conditions, but the rest took only ninety minutes. Cook's contribution was 111 not out. The stand established a plethora of records, the main ones being that Goonesena's score is still the highest for Cambridge in the fixture, and that the stand is the highest for any wicket in the Varsity Match. After such a demoralising passage of play, Oxford offered little resistance a second time around, conceding defeat by an innings and 186 runs, another record for Cambridge in the match. Fittingly, it was Goonesena, captain in his final season, that wrapped it up with four wickets, taking his tally for Cambridge to over 200, to go with his 2,000 runs, a unique double in the annals of university cricket.

The close season was marred by tragedy when Brian Swift, wicketkeeper in 1957, was killed in a car crash, and 1958 itself was a financial disappointment, with a deficit of £1,600. This was partly due to a small allocation from the MCC, but the situation was eased somewhat in 1959 when, for the first time, £2,000 was allocated to the Club regardless of the take from Test matches. On the other side of the coin, the first day of the Varsity Match was moved from Saturday to Wednesday, a sign of the

Gamini Goonesena, holder of the unique double of 2,000 runs and 200 wickets for Cambridge.

slow drop in its standing as a social occasion, while the Athletics Club shifted its centre of operations to a new track on Milton Road. Suddenly, some harsh truths had to be faced if the Club was to remain viable in the long term. In fact, the most that happened was that the University Hockey Club was invited to use the ground in the winter, a move that was not enough to offset the loss of the Athletics Club. It soon became apparent that the Cricket Club would have to pay the groundstaff out of its own pocket, a situation that lasted into the 1960s, when the ground was leased to the University in return for it picking up the wages bill.

On the field, the most significant achievement was a 99-run victory in the 1958 Varsity Match, led from the front by skipper Ted Dexter. After a rapid 58 in Cambridge's second innings, he took four for 14 as Oxford's resistance crumbled on the final day. Otherwise, Wheatley's eighty wickets in the season created a new record for either University, but such individual brilliance was not enough on its own. Over the two seasons, there were no wins against the counties, and in 1959 the Club suffered no less than fourteen losses. It was becoming hard to justify a programme of nineteen matches, either financially or in terms of overall playing strength. On the other hand, Fenner's was still a great nursery for young batsmen in particular, and there certainly seemed no immediate reason for abandoning first-class status altogether.

The athletics track could still be seen after its use had ceased.

THIRTEEN

FROM BREARLEY
TO PRINGLE

If the 1960s was a time of great social upheaval, this was certainly reflected in cricket, starting with the abolition of amateur status in 1962. Suddenly Oxford and Cambridge were the last bastions of the gentleman cricketer in the first-class game, and how much longer would they be a part of that set-up? The pace of modern life also meant that people no longer had the time to devote to a game that was becoming increasingly dull, a fact illustrated perfectly by the Varsity Match, where by the middle of the decade attendances had dwindled to no more than 2,000 paying spectators over the three days. A sequence of six draws in a row did not help, although to be fair there were some exciting finishes to savour.

Crowds wanted instant entertainment, and they were given it in 1963 with the inauguration of the Gillette Cup. Even Cambridge caught the mood of the moment, with a series of one-day matches against the International Cavaliers at Fenner's. With all these changes, it was comforting to know that for the time being at least, there were still some Cambridge dons who considered contributions to College and University just as important as academic achievement. Tony Lewis relates how, having been recommended by his Glamorgan captain Wilf Wooller, his admissions interview with the senior tutor of Christ's College consisted of questions about his family and some useful rugby coaching tips. So, there was still hope after all!

1960 promised more than subsequent years could deliver, with three county victories, including two at Fenner's. The most exciting finish was against Somerset, when, after Lewis and Roger Prideaux, another future England player, had compiled a century opening stand in each innings, 4 runs were still needed off the last over. Cambridge scrambled home, but it was a different story in the Varsity Match, against one of the most powerful Oxford sides for years. It was all they could do to hang on for a draw, thanks largely to Lewis' 95. Two of his compatriots, Dai and Emrys Davies, were officiating, and they were free with their advice as the young tyro

Mike Brearley, Cambridge's most prolific batsman, with 4,310 runs.

approached his century. He repaid them by dancing down the pitch and holing out to mid-on, much to the fury of Dai Davies. At least he made up for it in 1962, finally registering three figures at his last attempt. Another England captain, Mike Brearley, also made a hundred in that match, but it could not prevent the game meandering to another draw.

The brainpower of the Cambridge team was considerably enhanced by two freshers in 1961, and fortunately they also proved to be outstanding University cricketers. Eddie Craig was, according to *Wisden*, the first cricketer in fifty years to obtain a First in three triposes, and Brearley achieved a First in Classics and an Upper Second in Moral Sciences. Brearley was wicketkeeper in his first year, and Craig would stand at first slip trading philosophical niceties designed to bewilder teammates and opposition alike. Not only that, they both managed to score 1,300 runs in a Cambridge season, as did Prideaux and Lewis, the latter twice. Brearley finished at Cambridge with a new record of 4,310 runs, but he did have nearly twice as many innings as David Sheppard, who rests a secure second on the list of top runscorers. The bowling that year was also strengthened by the addition of Tony Pearson from Downside, fast-medium with an occasionally devastating out-swinger, as he demonstrated against Leicestershire with the first all-ten wicket haul for Cambridge since Sammy Woods. This match was the only county win of the season, and was, apart from a triumph against Nottinghamshire in 1963, the last such victory until the 1970s.

The 1963 side to play Oxford.

The batting line-up of that 1963 side was especially impressive, for after Craig and Brearley there came Richard Hutton, son of Sir Leonard and a good enough all-rounder to represent England, and Ray White, a hard-hitting South African who played with some success for Gloucestershire and Transvaal. The middle order was completed by another son of an England player, Mike Griffith, future captain of Sussex and an England hockey player, and Tony Windows, another Gloucestershire stalwart, and promising enough to be picked to tour Pakistan with the MCC under-25 team in 1966. Indeed, nine of the team that took to the field against Oxford that year played county cricket, compared with only four twenty years later. So in a way these were still golden days for university cricket, despite the lack of tangible success; yet the second half of the decade saw Cambridge plunging to new depths from which, in the last forty years, it has only intermittently managed to rise.

At least Cambridge's long-suffering cricket lovers had the pleasure of observing the leadership style of England's most successful post-war captain at close quarters for two successive seasons. *Wisden* was unusually effusive about this Renaissance man:

Brearley delighted his admirers not only by the number of runs he obtained, but the manner in which he scored them. He displayed splendid concentration and was continually on the look out for scoring opportunities. He impressed equally as much as captain, as was proved when he was appointed to lead the President of MCC's XI against the Australians. Brearley's sporting qualities in no way interfered with his studies and his academic career included a double-first and first place in the Home Civil Service examination.

The 1964 season finished on an even greater high with selection for England's tour of South Africa, but in the end Brearley had to wait until 1976 for his first cap. At one stage it seemed that academia might prove too strong a call, as it had for Craig, who became a fellow of Churchill College. He returned to Cambridge in 1966 for postgraduate studies, playing two matches to give Deryck Murray's team a helping hand, but decided to put his serious work on hold for the more frivolous life of a cricketer, a decision for which Ian Botham in particular will be eternally grateful.

Murray came up to Cambridge having already kept wicket for the West Indies, and first played under Ray White's leadership in 1965. That year he and White helped embarrass the New Zealanders, who were forced to follow on after Cambridge had scored 364. White scored 151, showing his very best form, as described by Jack Davies:

On such occasions it seems to be beyond the capacity of any bowler to produce a delivery to which he cannot react with an attacking stroke. The crispness of his timing is such that the fielders have scarcely moved before the ball is past them. The new ball is not a fresh weapon in the hand of the bowler, merely something to be seen more clearly than the old. Even Dexter and May seldom attacked with such devastating vigour.

The New Zealanders played out time easily enough, and regrettably White only scored two more hundreds in another ninety-five innings for Cambridge, a disappointing return for one so massively talented.

Murray took over the captaincy in 1966, but, sadly, he proved to be one of the Club's least inspirational captains:

The barrel, for the time being, has clearly run dry… the season got off to a controversial start when the captain… announced that he would select the team only from those who had made themselves available during the term.

Thus, thanks to a decision that was severely myopic given the increasing demands on students in the summer term, Cambridge arrived at Lord's minus several useful performers. The result was a crushing innings defeat, the only positive result of the decade. Indeed, in all games, the only victory between 1965 and 1969 was against a weak Scottish side. The only sign of recovery, as the sixties thankfully came to an end, was the arrival of Dudley Owen-Thomas from KCS Wimbledon. His 182 not out against Middlesex in 1969 was the most stirring innings of the whole decade, and a welcome boost to those who had waited too long for a resurgence in the Club's fortunes.

Revival came quicker than anyone could have hoped in the shape of Majid Jahangir Khan, son of the great Cambridge all-rounder of the 1930s. Cyril Coote

Majid Khan rests from his labours.

remembered his father with great affection, and often told the tale of how, from the top of the pavilion steps, he threw down the stumps out in the centre of the square. Majid never quite managed this, but it was just about the only thing he didn't achieve in three glorious years. He was already a mature cricketer when he came up, having played for Pakistan and helped Glamorgan to its second County Championship win in 1969. Not since Duleepsinhji had one man created such a stir in Cambridge, and once again lecture theatres started to empty when news got round that Majid had gone in to bat. And it wasn't just the technical and aesthetic brilliance of his batting that made such an impact; through his words and deeds he managed to inspire those around him in a manner not matched at Cambridge in the twentieth century. Captained by Tony Jorden, a future England rugby full-back, the squad looked far more competitive, even though results were only slightly improved. The attack was strengthened by the addition of John Spencer, later a great Sussex stalwart, and by the increased use of the medium-pace of Roger Knight, in his final year before a successful playing and administrative career. The one victory was, ironically, against Glamorgan, captained by a sympathetic Tony Lewis. His declaration, leaving Cambridge 292 to make in 330 minutes, was a generous one, and Majid made sure the opportunity was not squandered. His century was one of the five he made during the season, culminating in a magnificent 200 against Oxford. To Cambridge's deep chagrin, rain prevented a finish, but at least there were many reasons to be positive, 1,216 of them coming from the magical blade of Majid Khan.

The Victorian pavilion, in need of a restoration that never came.

Over the weekend of the Glamorgan match, there had been a disturbing incident, as reported in the *Cambridge Evening News*:

When the players arrived this morning to resume the match they found food had been thrown all over the refreshment tent and some of the beer had been drunk. The thieves smashed the pavilion door, drank more beer and ransacked the dressing rooms. But all they got away with was a small amount of petty cash and a few coins from the public phone box, which they ripped open. Most of the players had removed their kit from the dressing rooms.

Very sensible. The farcical conclusion to the break-in seemed symbolic of the decaying state of the pavilion, with its splintery floorboards and inadequate changing facilities. Indeed, it was nearing the end of its glorious existence. In its wisdom, the committee had proposed in 1966 that funds for a new building should be found from the sale of the garden on the Gresham Road frontage and of the site of the existing pavilion. Work finally began on the building, at the Hughes Hall end of the ground, in October 1971. It was valued at £39,900, and was designed by former Blue Colin Stansfield-Smith. It has been difficult for members to warm to this more functional edifice, which would perhaps be more at home on a Scandinavian seafront than a first-class cricket ground. Meanwhile, the elegant Victorian pavilion was pulled down, and some of its contents auctioned off, including the clock, currently owned by Tony Lewis. If only it could have been spared for a few more years, the old pavilion would have been listed and quite possibly voted for in a reality TV programme. Either way, Fenner's would still have its greatest asset, just as Oxford has preserved its own distinctive building in The Parks.

The Cambridge side of 1971 ranks with some of the classic line-ups of the past as one of the best ever. Although not quite having the record of the 1878 and 1921 teams, with three wins and four losses in ten games, it can justifiably claim to be the finest all-round side since the war. The attack was easily of county standard, with Sussex's John Spencer joined by seamer Mike Selvey, who had already played for Surrey, slow left-armer Philippe Edmonds (later Selvey's teammate at Middlesex) and Robert Hadley, a fast bowler on Glamorgan's books. Aside from Majid, this year's inspirational captain, the batting included Owen-Thomas, Young Cricketer of the Year in 1972, and Peter Johnson, who had enjoyed a brilliant career at Nottingham High School. Overall, a finely balanced side, and, as *Wisden* said 'cold figures did scant justice to Cambridge cricket in 1971'.

This was a turbulent year on the subcontinent, with war not only in Kashmir, but also between East and West Pakistan over the East's bid for independence, a conflict that ended with the creation of Bangladesh. When the Pakistani team arrived at Fenner's near the beginning of its tour of England, it was greeted by a ring of over 200 policemen outside the ground. They were anticipating a large crowd of Eastern Pakistanis and student demonstrators objecting to the presence of West Pakistanis. As it turned out, the organisers were to be disappointed, as less than fifty actually turned up, and most of the police were sent home at lunch time.

On the pitch, the first day saw plenty of incident. Pakistan batted first in humid conditions, and was soon in trouble as Spencer took a wicket in each of his first two overs. Zaheer and Asif rallied somewhat, but Spencer returned to roll over the tail and the innings was over in only 140 minutes. Majid and Owen-Thomas then put the tourists' poor display into context by adding 145 in 129 minutes for the second wicket before bad light stopped play for the day twenty-five minutes early. Already 67 ahead overnight, Cambridge could afford not to be unduly concerned by a morning in which they only scored 47 runs for the loss of five wickets. Still, play needed enlivening, and that is precisely what New Zealand rugby Blue Howard Steele did with three sixes in the afternoon session. Cambridge had a startling lead of 234.

Hadley struck twice in an over to start the rot a second time, and although Zaheer and Asif again played some cultured strokes, only Wasim Bari showed the requisite concentration in an innings of two-and-three-quarter hours. When Spencer finished it with a caught and bowled, the end was in sight. Asif Masood struck a couple of well-aimed blows to avoid the ignominy of an innings defeat, but only two were required for a famous Cambridge victory. Who but John Spencer, promoted by Majid, should hit the winning runs off the first ball? It was only the sixth win by Cambridge over a touring team from overseas, and the first since 1927. The euphoria was increased by reports that young Imran Khan, injured for this game but on his first tour of England, was likely to join Cambridge in 1972. Unfortunately, the rumour was only half true – he ended up at Oxford!

Fenner's in 1972, by local artist Lewis Todd. Try to find the eleventh fielder.

A new limited-over competition was introduced in 1972, and there was much excitement at Fenner's when it was decided that Cambridge should represent the Universities in the first year of the Benson & Hedges Cup, with Oxford having its turn in 1973. It was predicted that Cambridge would be strong enough on its own to challenge the might of the counties, but the Light Blues underperformed and lost all four zonal games, despite John Spencer's four for 29 in the first home match against Worcestershire. Indeed, the whole season was a disappointment after the previous year's triumphs, with no wins and three losses in the seven games prior to the Varsity Match. Despite the successes of 1971, this was one win that eluded Cambridge, Oxford hanging on desperately for a draw. The record needed to be set straight, as the last time Cambridge had won was in 1958 under Ted Dexter.

As so often, the University Match was played against the backdrop of the Wimbledon fortnight, and the papers were full of the fledgling romance between teenagers Jimmy Connors and Chris Evert, although their mothers insisted they were just good friends. None of this would have worried Majid Khan in his last first-class game for Cambridge and openers Hodson and Snowden treated the occasion with due seriousness when they went out to bat. They scored just 16 in the first thirty minutes, all of them behind the wicket. The 50 came up in 107 minutes, but when Hodson was out, the tempo immediately increased. Although Majid didn't stay long, Owen-Thomas soon took a liking to the Oxford bowling, hitting eleven fours in his first 50. He found a willing ally in Steele, who hit Wagstaffe for two sixes over mid-wicket, and helped add 85 at a run a minute. When Majid declared late in the day, Owen-Thomas had batted for three hours and twenty-five minutes, and hit twenty-two fours. He had also joined the select band of those who had scored more than one century against Oxford, after a magnificent 146 the year before. Majid knew that Oxford would not enjoy batting against Spencer and Hadley on the lively Lord's pitch, but he did not know quite how little. By the close, the scored stood at 4 for 4, which became 10 for six the next morning when Hadley removed Faber's middle stump. 32 was the lowest score ever in the Varsity match, and that seemed a long way off as Lee joined Hamblin. Fortunately for Oxford, common sense finally prevailed, and with only three men in front of the wicket, they were able to combine dogged defence with some face-saving boundaries. After the 50 stand came up in 72 minutes, Hadley was recalled, and soon got rid of Lee, effectively ending Oxford's resistance. Following on 159 behind, the Oxford batsmen again found the extra bounce and movement too much to handle, and they limped to 89 for seven at the end of the second day. They survived for an hour-and-a-half the next day before Kinkead-Weekes, having just hooked Kendall for six, skied him to Majid attempting to repeat the shot. A fitting end to the University career of one of the most charismatic cricketers to emerge from Cambridge since the Second World War, and the close of a particularly memorable chapter at Fenner's. Would his like be seen again? Probably not, and there is no doubt that he is still the most exciting talent seen in the ancient university town in the last fifty years.

Phil Edmonds took over the captaincy in 1973, and while he too led from the front, he was severely hampered by the loss of six key Blues. There was only one close county match, a two-wicket loss against Kent, but there was some comfort taken from the fact that six Light Blues were selected for the first ever combined Oxford and Cambridge team, for the match against New Zealand. Although it was another sign of the decline in strength of university cricket, Edmonds almost inspired his charges to achieve a remarkable victory; at the close, the students only needed 4 more to win with nine wickets down. Oxford created a stir by becoming the first non-county side to win a game in the Benson & Hedges Cup, but after a disastrous showing by Cambridge in 1974, the authorities bowed to the inevitable by insisting on a combined team from 1975.

The Varsity Match had settled into a familiar pattern of tailenders playing out time, although the 1975 match rose above the ordinary with a fine fourth-wicket stand of 161 in 140 minutes between two promising freshers, Peter Roebuck and Alastair Hignell. Roebuck had arrived from Millfield, where his parents were both teachers, with a burgeoning reputation, while Hignell was known better for his outstanding record as a rugby full-back. Indeed, his first appearance at Fenner's was delayed due to his selection for England's off-season tour of Australia. The other noteworthy incident in that game was the first case of concussion in the Varsity Match, inflicted on wicketkeeper Steve Coverdale by a rampant Imran Khan. Fortunately, being a Yorkshireman, Coverdale was tough enough to return in the second innings to save the match for Cambridge. However, with the exception of these doughty characters, *Wisden's* correspondent was unimpressed by the products of the modern educational system:

Why we all love the '70s. Alastair Hignell in the nets!

The basic fault… lies with the schools and, although there are signs that improvements are being made in this direction, university cricket will not improve as much as it should until players arrive better coached in the basic arts.

Regrettably, the scribe had identified a trend that has continued ever since, although very recently there seems finally to have been a recognition once again of the importance of team games, including cricket, in a full curriculum.

1975 also marked the end of the Victorian regulations governing university cricket. The changes meant that any student in residence could play for the eleven, a ruling that enabled Oxford's Roger Moulding to obtain his Blue no less than six years in a row. The new regulation was subtly amended in 1982 to allow only those paying fees and studying while in residence to be awarded a Blue. Another first occurred in 1976 when David Jarrett, who had played for Oxford in 1975, switched allegiance the very next year. Cambridge had reason to be thankful for his decision, as he held a strong Oxford attack at bay for over three hours in its second innings. He was helped in the rearguard action by Stephen Wookey, who himself played for Oxford in 1978, but this time Cambridge's luck finally ran out as Oxford cantered home by ten wickets.

If ever a career was launched by a single innings, it was that of Paul Parker at Fenner's in April of that year. With his team facing the possibility of an innings defeat, he stayed for almost a whole day in compiling an elegant 215, which included twenty-eight fours and two sixes. He went on to score two more hundreds in the Cambridge season, finishing with nearly 700 runs scored in a manner that presaged well for the future. He later enjoyed a highly successful career with Sussex, and was rewarded with a token England cap at The Oval in 1981. Not only was Parker's future secured by that memorable innings, but as fellow student Shaun Mundy recounts:

At the end of his innings on the third day, Scyld Berry and I composed, and phoned in to the Telegraph, *an article summarising the day's play – and particularly Paul's innings. An article duly appeared in the following day's* Telegraph, *under the byline 'By a Special Correspondent', though it bore relatively limited resemblance to the article we had composed. I think that this was Scyld's first venture into newsprint.*

Even if admission tutors' doors were rapidly being closed on potential student cricketers, there was still room for the use of initiative in the wider world, as Berry's subsequent journalistic success has proved.

The Cambridge team of 1978 was dominated by rugby players: in addition to Hignell, Matthew Fosh, Ian Peck and Ian Greig all obtained their Blues for the sport, while Parker would have done but for injury. Unfortunately, according to *Wisden*, none of them 'truly realised his full potential' at cricket in a soggy start to the summer. Seven of the nine games were drawn, including the Varsity Match, which lost nearly half its playing time to the weather. The attack once again proved not strong enough to breach county defences, although it came close against Surrey.

The county had sent a near full strength side, and Cambridge looked as though it would suffer heavily from the absence of Greig and Parker in the exam room. A lot rested on the shoulders of Hignell, captain for a second year after a winless but seriously rain-affected season in 1977. So it proved, as, after winning the toss, he had to steer his side through to lunch at a precarious 103 for five. Fosh had promised much, adding 58 in only thirty-nine minutes with Hignell before Payne castled him. Hignell proceeded on his merry way after the break, helped by Mike Howat, son of cricket writer Gerald. The captain reached an aggressive hundred in only 145 minutes, with thirteen fours, but resistance ended with his demise.

At 105 for one overnight, Surrey never looked like losing another wicket as the second day wore on. Roger Knight spared the undergraduates any more punishment by declaring halfway through the afternoon, and at one stage it was doubtful whether Cambridge would last the day after Baker had taken the first three wickets cheaply. Hignell finally found a worthy companion in Neil Crawford, a seam bowler from Shrewsbury. Perhaps he was a little too circumspect, getting stuck for an hour on 2, but Hignell's crashing strokeplay made up for it, and the close was reached at 138 for three. Although Crawford departed early the next day, Jim Dewes, son of the legendary John, stayed with Hignell while 98 were added in just fifty-eight minutes. 'Wielding his bat like a broadsword', Hignell only needed seventy-five minutes to move from his overnight 78 to 145. He was then caught off a skier on the long-on boundary, having batted for 175 minutes and hit twenty-three fours and a six. He thus became the first batsman to hit a century in each innings for Cambridge since Roger Prideaux in 1960. Suddenly there was talk of Cambridge causing an upset.

Surrey needed 193 to win in about three hours on a pitch beginning to take some turn, and after a shaky start Mark Allbrook of Nottinghamshire began to exploit the batsmen's doubts with his accurate off-spin. Disaster struck after he had taken four quick wickets, as he was forced to leave the field. Despite Hignell's experiments with his own special brand of leg-spin, Knight and Jackman held out, and the hero of the hour was left to reflect on what might have been.

One notable victory that year was in a non first-class game, but one that had become a regular and competitive fixture. David Beaumont, a thirty-two-year-old policeman from Nottingham, who was to become Wolfson College's first cricket Blue, describes the occasion:

The most interesting game was against D.H. Robins' XI. This was not a first-class fixture but when you see his side it makes you wonder. It consisted of Allan Lamb, Allan Border, Peter Kirsten, Imran Khan, Garth Le Roux, Henry Fotheringham, Peter Parfitt (captain), Tim Head and two Gloucestershire players and one Indian. They only lost eight wickets in the whole match but then lost the game when we had to score 330 on the last day and we all got 50 or more. I actually scored 48 not out and then hit the winning six but the scorer credited it to Paul Parker. We had a scorer, P.J. Batten, who used the Frindall Book and no one knew how to score when he went off on the third day to get his degree!

This was Alastair Hignell's last year at Cambridge, as it was for Matthew Fosh and Paul Parker. Two more than adequate replacements were found, however, in Derek Pringle from Felsted and David Surridge from Hertfordshire, who later opened the bowling for Gloucestershire. The batting may not have been quite as strong as in 1978, but the seam attack was much the best since the Majid Khan era. Regrettably, this still did not translate into results, with two losses and seven draws coming into the University match. Five of the previous six meetings had been drawn, and Cambridge had last won the fixture seven years before. Their bowling gave them the edge, though, and if the weather was kind it was their best chance for years.

Ian Greig would have batted if he had won the toss on a heavy, overcast morning, but as it was the Oxford captain beat him to it and took first strike. It soon proved to be a handy toss to lose, as Greig himself dismissed his opposite number and then Roger Moulding in the space of three balls. Surridge was also outstanding, taking three wickets in a fiery spell that left Oxford lunching uneasily at 81 for six. The afternoon session saw Oxford batsmen reprieved on four occasions, but it didn't seem to matter as Pringle kept up the pressure. Poor technique, allied to accurate and probing bowling ensured, that the innings lasted only forty-one overs, the last four wickets falling after lunch for just 16.

The sun broke through the London haze when Cambridge batted, and Nick Cooper of Gloucestershire took the opportunity to set out his stall for a long innings. He showed his limpet-like qualities by staying for the fifty overs left that day, scoring 47 out of 131 for four. Nigel Popplewell, son of High Court judge and former Cambridge wicketkeeper Sir Oliver, celebrated the award of a Somerset contract by livening things up with a quick 40 before falling in the day's last over.

The next morning, Pringle continued this more positive approach, duly reaching his 50 before lunch. Afterwards, conscious of the need to expedite a declaration, and rapidly losing partners, he decided to have a bit of a slog. On 91, he danced down the wicket to Hameed, smiting him for six over mid-wicket. On 99, he went through the agonies of watching Surridge play out five balls, but next over he reached his maiden first-class hundred, and Greig immediately declared. The runs had come in 187 minutes, and he hit eight fours and three sixes. It had been the kind of innings that England fans would have wanted him to play, but sadly his batting never reached such heights in a Test match.

Greig, diagnosed with a broken bone in his wrist, still managed to take two wickets and two sharp slip catches before resting, and Oxford slumped almost as badly as in the first innings. At 109 for six at the end of the second day, the last four wickets only took another hour to acquire in the morning. An innings victory was just reward for a far superior side, and suddenly there was a real sense of optimism that a new era had arrived.

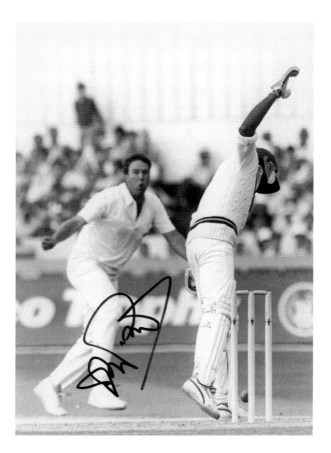

Derek Pringle troubles Jeff Dujon with the sort of extra bounce that made him a handful at Fenner's.

FOURTEEN

THE LAST STAND

If 1979 was a good bowling team, that of 1982 was extremely strong in batting, with, in addition to Pringle, David Varey, later of Lancashire, Robin Boyd-Moss of Northamptonshire and Stephen Henderson of Worcestershire, who scored a double-hundred against Middlesex in this, his first year. Boyd-Moss also notched a century in each innings against Warwickshire, but Pringle was the star, the biggest draw in Cambridge cricket since Majid Khan. Unable to bowl at the start of the season due to an ankle injury sustained in pre-season practice, he piled on the runs, scoring 521 runs in only six games at an average of 74. This followed a fine all-round season in 1980, when he scored 604 runs and took twenty-four wickets. Regrettably, that year's Varsity Match was ruined by the weather, and that of 1981 by an unadventurous declaration by Oxford.

Victory against a county was still elusive, and Cambridge was yet to bowl a side out when Lancashire visited Fenner's. The good news was that Pringle was fit to bowl again, and on the front pages there was relief that thirteen Cambridge scientists had finally arrived home after being trapped in South Georgia at the start of the Falklands conflict. Cambridge's captain made a promising start when Lancashire batted, removing Abrahams and Hayes in the same over. The two Davids, Lloyd and Hughes, restored order in a fourth-wicket stand that took Lancashire into lunch at 135 for three.

Pringle was no-balled twelve times before the interval, and nineteen times in total, but overall he must have been pleased with his and his teammates' performance. They bowled out the opposition for the first time that term in just over eighty overs, allowing time for Mills and Boyd-Moss to play themselves in before the close, which arrived at a promising 56 for one. Hopes of a first-innings lead were soon shattered in the morning, as debutant left-armer Ian Folley took four quick wickets, including Pringle. A score of 164 for six at lunch was disappointing, but Hodgson and Pollock put on 64 for the seventh wicket to keep Cambridge in the fight. Lancashire hoped

Simon Henderson hits the winning runs against Lancashire in 1982.

a lead of 30 would be adequate, but a sensational collapse ensued, Pringle taking five of the six wickets to fall that night for 70. The pitch was certainly becoming more difficult to bat on, as David Lloyd, never one to shy away from controversy, was quick to point out. David Hallett reported:

On inspection at the close it was clear that, in one tiny spot, the top had indeed gone but when I approached county skipper David Lloyd the conversation went something like this: 'I see the top has gone in one tiny spot.' 'Yes', he replied: 'One spot about a yard square.'… I suspect that much of the damage to the area at the Gresham Road end of the pitch was done by successive county batsmen pounding the spot with their bats.

Charlie Ellison, brother of Kent's Richard, helped Pringle complete the carnage the next day, and when the players came off twenty-five minutes before lunch, Pringle's pleasure was enhanced by the news of his call-up for the MCC game against India a week later. Liberated by the selectors' faith in him, Pringle turned the match around after tea, adding 87 in just fifty minutes with Henderson to see Cambridge home with well over an hour to spare. The first win against a county for eleven years was thoroughly deserved, or as David Lloyd put it: 'Pringle excelled, but so he should'. Whatever help there was in the pitch, the Lancashire bowlers hadn't found it, and Pringle's reputation as one of the most influential Cambridge players of recent years was established for all to see.

The selectors liked what they saw so much that they decided to pick Pringle for the opening Test of the summer, making him the first Cambridge Blue to be picked for England while still an undergraduate since Peter May in 1951. As Chairman of Selectors, May had a special interest in Pringle's future, and indeed there were some rumblings about the picking of what was perceived as a product of the old-boy network. In the event, Pringle justified his selection with four wickets in a seven-wicket win over India, but this only created another dilemma, both for him and the selectors. The Second Test clashed with the Varsity Match, and in May's time it would have been unthinkable for a student to miss the chance of a Blue for something as trivial as a Test. He therefore gave Pringle the chance to miss the next game, reassuring him that if he did it would in no way jeopardise his England career. As recently as 1971, Majid Khan had declined an invitation to play for Pakistan in favour of representing Cambridge at Lord's, but Pringle had different ideas:

'Captaining Cambridge in the Varsity Match would have been a great honour, but I am a professional cricketer now and obviously the biggest prize is to play for one's country.'

Whatever the rights and wrongs of the situation, Pringle's amateur brethren were left to pick up the pieces. Peter Mills, whose career had hitherto been chiefly distinguished by being dismissed by the very first ball of the 1981 season, took over the captaincy. He thus became the first son of a Cambridge captain to lead the team against Oxford, as his father had in 1948. In a game of declarations, his team was left 272 to win in 210 minutes, a challenging target. It was made possible by a blazing hundred by Boyd-Moss, assisted by Henderson in a partnership of 144 in twenty-two overs. The former's century came in just 100 minutes, probably the quickest for Cambridge in the match's history, and it was enough to set up a memorable seven-wicket win. His teammates needed little encouragement to quaff the champagne that Pringle had sent down for the occasion. He must have felt a pang of jealousy, as England's game was a washout, and he was struggling to make an impact at the highest level.

Boyd-Moss was at it again next year, becoming the first batsman to score a century in each innings in the Varsity Match, as well as the first to score three hundreds in successive innings. Cambridge's opening salvo was further fortified by a second-wicket stand of 215 between Boyd-Moss and Worcestershire's Tim Curtis, a Cambridge record for the match. It was not enough to produce a positive result, and in 1984, with Boyd-Moss and Henderson no longer around to prop up the middle order, Cambridge slid to a five-wicket defeat against the old enemy. The 1985 match was equally one-sided, although ultimately undecided despite Oxford's Giles Toogood becoming the first Englishman to perform the match double in nearly 160 years of the fixture. Rob Andrew, England's most distinguished fly half until Johnny Wilkinson came along, was captain of a moderate side that year, and victories, even against Oxford, seemed a remote prospect.

1986 saw a particularly wet term at Fenner's, which did not help groundsman Tony Pocock in his preparation. Nevertheless, the TCCB Inspector of Pitches was called in after complaints about the state of the square, and recommended remedial works be done during the close season to a pitch that was increasingly slow and low. In all, Cambridge had lost one and drawn six of its preliminary games, not bad for a team lacking star quality. Charlie Ellison was back to bolster the attack, and he was

Cambridge contributed only four players to the side that beat Gloucestershire in 1984.

joined in a strong seam department by John Davidson from Aberystwyth and left-armer Alastair Scott, who played one game for Sussex at the end of the season.

The sun was still largely absent on the big day at Lord's, influencing David Price's decision to insert Oxford. The Dark Blues found it heavy going, but could be satisfied with their morning's work, reaching lunch at 87 for two. The afternoon belonged to the captain David Thorne, already on Warwickshire's books, and playing here as though his life depended on it. However, 163 for five at tea became 167 all out as Davidson took four for 13 in just twenty-five balls. Advantage Cambridge. Cambridge passed the modest Oxford total just after lunch on the second day, by which time freshman Paul Bail from Millfield had moved to his maiden first-class hundred off just 165 balls. By the time he was out for the seventh highest score in the Varsity Match, he had hit two sixes and twenty fours in an innings of great freedom. Some late order hitting from Andrew Golding and Davidson ensured that Bail's effort wasn't wasted, allowing Price to declare just before the close with a lead of 163.

The next day, Hagan and Kilborn batted stubbornly, and then Thorne more convincingly, to lead Oxford on the road to safety, taking lunch at 121 for two. Thorne carried on in the same vein afterwards, reaching his hundred in three hours, but wickets were tumbling at the other end. Still, at the start of the last twenty overs Oxford was 104 ahead with two wickets left, with a draw the most likely option.

Michael Atherton in the slips against Middlesex in 1988.

Davidson and Scott had other ideas, taking the last two wickets in just eleven balls. Cambridge wanted 106 from sixteen overs, a tall but not impossible task. 51 from six became 30 from the last three – surely a few too many? Davidson, fresh from nine wickets in the match, was promoted and swung lustily to bring things down to the wire. When he was run out off the fourth ball of the last over, four were still needed. Rutnagur now gave Cambridge the advantage by bowling a wide, and David Browne managed two off the next ball. The last ball ended the match in classical fashion as Golding and Browne scampered a leg bye to snatch an unlikely victory. As Doug Insole, at Lord's on behalf of the ICC, put it with just a touch of understatement: 'It certainly brightened up a heavy committee meeting'.

As the 1980s came to an end, the gulf between the universities and the counties was growing ever more apparent, and Cambridge victories were as rare as hens' teeth. Yet all was not doom and gloom, as this period saw the emergence of two future England openers, Mike Atherton and Steve James, and a wicketkeeper in Rob Turner not far short of international class. Atherton and James were so far ahead of their contemporaries that they seemed at times to be saving games single-handedly, but in truth their efforts inspired lesser mortals to greater heights. Atherton had scored the only Cambridge century of the 1987 season and had ended with over 1,000 runs altogether, also appearing for Lancashire. Destiny seemed to await when Atherton was given the captaincy for his second season. Only just twenty, he was the youngest Cambridge captain of the century. He found an effective opening bowler in Nigel Fenton from Rugby School, and Alastair Scott returned from his desk in the City to help out for a few games. This time, Atherton was head and shoulders above his peers, scoring 665 runs with an average of 60. He had five scores of over fifty, a landmark only reached once by any other Cambridge player in eight games.

Pitches at Fenner's were generally helpful to bowlers in 1988, and Atherton was content to bowl first on winning the toss against Middlesex. Scott took four good wickets, but some slogging from Simon Hughes and Andy Needham ensured a respectable total. Even so, Atherton must have been quite happy with his decision. Once again he played a lone hand, scoring a hundred out of 169 for seven. His dour reputation was already established, at least among his teammates:

Alastair Scott, the deputed senior professional of the side, was dispatched with a note soon after Atherton had passed his previous best score of 110. Loosely translated, the missive suggested that they had been so bored by his four-hour hundred that they could only be appeased with champagne. The note finished with a request for a little brighter batting for the rest of his innings. 'That could be described as a liberal translation of what the note actually said', agreed Atherton.

Finding a partner whom he could trust to stay with him, Atherton supplied the fizz by completing his next 50 in just sixty-six balls. In all he had batted for 304 minutes, and hit a six and seventeen fours.

Sensibly declaring 25 behind, Cambridge removed Sykes and Carr before the close for only 31, setting up an intriguing last day. A surprise Cambridge victory was definitely on the cards as Middlesex slumped to 162 for eight with three hours left, but Olley and Fraser shut up shop and could not be budged despite Atherton trying his own leg-spinners. The crucial moment came when Neil Maclaurin, son of the future ECB Chairman, was dropped on 14 in his second and last first-class innings.

Roland Butcher declared at tea, leaving an unlikely target of 221 in an hour plus twenty overs. Atherton hadn't given up just yet, promoting the hard-hitting Atkinson to open with Turner. Although they managed 45 in the first nine overs, Atherton recognised this still wasn't enough and ordered some batting practice. 'A moral victory' declared the headline that evening, a rare enough event, but Atherton's men could fairly claim that they were robbed by professionals who were too scared of losing to 'mere' amateurs. There was no chance of anyone winning or losing at the beginning of July, when the 144th Varsity Match became the first ever to be washed out without a ball being bowled. Quite rightly, all those who would have played were awarded their Blue.

Perhaps Atherton's finest hour as an undergraduate came in 1989 as captain of the Combined Universities team in the Benson & Hedges Cup. With two wins in the zonal games it became the first non-county side to reach the quarter-finals. As it was no longer confined to Oxford and Cambridge players, the team included cricketers of the quality of Nasser Hussain for its trip to Taunton. Unfortunately, one Cambridge player was not so lucky, as David Hallett recalls:

Steve James wasn't allowed to go, although he was only doing term exams. Durham had four players doing finals, but they were allowed to travel down with tutors.

The students missed a semi-final berth by a whisker after a brilliant hundred by Hussain, but James' predicament was more worrying in the longer term for Cambridge's future.

In June 1990, England was about to embark on its most important football game since 1966 and batsmen across the country, including England's new recruit Michael Atherton, made hay while the sun shone in a record-breaking summer. University batsmen didn't want to miss out on the party, John Crawley's brother Mark averaging 88 for Oxford and Steve James scoring over 700 runs for Cambridge, with three hundreds. Success was still proving elusive, however, with four draws and four losses by the end of June. There was one more chance to warm up before the annual trip to headquarters.

The *Evening News* deemed the game between Cambridgeshire and Lincolnshire more worthy of coverage than Cambridge's match, a sign of the increasing frustration at the students' failure to beat a county since 1982. Sussex did nothing to suggest that sequence would end after being put in by Jonathan Atkinson of Somerset. After the early loss of Hall, one of seven uncapped players in the side, Lenham, Greenfield and Wells gorged themselves on some friendly bowling. Wells was particularly severe on Alan Buzza, the previous winter's rugby captain, and finished with twenty fours and two sixes. James, Heap and Turner gave Cambridge a solid start in reply, but once the second wicket fell at 171 no one took advantage of the placid track, and Atkinson was forced to declare 91 behind. Paul Parker instructed his troops to get a move on, and just over two hours later he was able to set Cambridge 256 to win in a minimum of sixty-one overs. If Middlesex had been over-cautious two years before, Parker might have been erring on the generous side, but he knew that once the top order had gone the rest of the batting was brittle. First, though, there was the small matter of getting rid of Steve James, on a high after scoring a century in the defeat of the New Zealanders by a combined Oxford and Cambridge side.

Since Russell Heap had hurt his knee, Rob Turner was sent in to open with James, and they gave the team the right sort of start. The inexperienced Sussex attack then suffered in the face of a perfectly paced stand of 142 in thirty-five overs between James and Mark Lowrey from Radley. When they were finally separated, James had been in for 158 minutes for his fourth century of the season. Victory should still have been a relative formality, but panic set in as Atkinson and Pyman were run out in what had become a one-day style finish. As it turned out, it was fortunate that Heap had been held back, as he put the issue beyond doubt with a few judicious blows, ending with a six. Cambridge may have won a game in which it had only taken five wickets, but it was a worthy win nevertheless, ending with only seven balls to spare after a finely judged declaration. If only more county captains were as sympathetic to the broader needs of the game.

Unfortunately, there was no chance to test out whether this was just a flash in the pan, as the Varsity Match was ruined by rain for the third year running. 1991's game was also a damp disappointment, but at least there was an opportunity to see the latest product of Manchester Grammar School in action. John Crawley promised much as

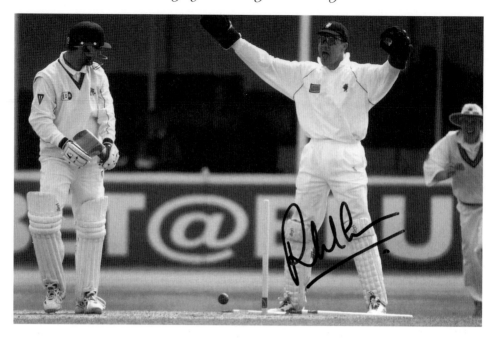

Above: *Rob Turner kept up the fine tradition of Cambridge stumpers.*

Left: *John Crawley played for England the year after leaving Cambridge in 1993.*

an undergraduate, and looked a ready replacement for Atherton in the top order. Yet while he was exceptionally consistent, he left the best until last, producing the really big scores he was capable of in his final year. Still, in 1992, his second year and first as captain, he managed to top the averages with 541 runs at an average of 38, and, just as importantly showed the kind of leadership skills that have led to speculation ever since as to whether he would follow further in Atherton's footsteps by becoming England captain. Crawley had a rather thin spread of talent at his disposal, especially as the side was weakened by the sending down of his older brother Peter and a shoulder injury to strike bowler Rory Jenkins. Nevertheless, Cambridge only lost two matches at Fenner's, and had contrived four respectable draws by the time an experimental Kent side arrived in Cambridge for the University's last home match of the season. As usual Cambridge was playing its three spinners, who between them took forty-six out of the sixty-eight wickets taken during the season.

Crawley won the toss, and as was becoming the custom, put Kent in to bat. David Fulton, making his debut, was removed early along with Mark Ealham, but there was to be no more success that day as Jonathan Longley and Richard Ellison enjoyed some easy runs. A tea-time storm brought proceedings to a premature end for the day at 192 for three. With three hours lost, Kent pressed on the next day, with Longley reaching his maiden hundred, and double hockey Blue Marcus Wight picking up three consolation wickets with his off-breaks. Steve Marsh's declaration opened the match up, but Cambridge was in danger of following on until wicketkeeper Jonathan Arscott, as so often, came to the rescue with a crucial 50. Still, Kent would have slept soundly in the knowledge that they were 147 ahead with nine wickets left at the end of the second day. They added another 133 in the morning session before Marsh declared again at lunchtime, dangling the carrot of 281 to win in seventy-two overs in front of the Cambridge batsmen. Cambridge took it steadily up until tea, when the score stood at 101 for three. Garri Jones had compiled a cautious 36 in 107 minutes, providing a springboard for the more dashing middle order. First Wight took advantage of the inexperienced Kent attack, scoring 61 in ninety-six minutes and adding 77 with John Carroll. Two more wickets fell quickly, bringing in the jovial Simon Johnson, Cambridge's last real hope.

There followed an epic seventh-wicket partnership of 82 in a mere fifty minutes, before Carroll fell agonisingly short of a maiden hundred. His 92 had taken just 124 balls. Cambridge could still contrive to lose, even with only four needed. Pitcher went straight away for 0, but Johnson soothed frayed nerves by driving Ealham for four. His 45 had come off only 39 balls, and Cambridge went to Lord's on a high. In another game of declarations, they won by seven wickets, Crawley scoring an unbeaten century and adding 166 for the fourth wicket with Wight, a stand that enabled them to reach a finely judged target of 238 in the fifty-first over. It also meant that the Light Blues had won two first-class matches for the first time since 1982.

There was some sadness in the off-season with the death of Jack Davies, who had overseen Cambridge cricket for nearly forty years from 1952. President during the

Majid Khan era, he had also masterminded the sale of land that led to the building of the current pavilion. He was, too, a great help to those with less experience of cricket bureaucracy, as Professor David Buckingham CBE, Club President at the time of writing recalls:

Jack asked me if I could become involved, and he got me a place on the committee. When I became senior treasurer, Jack, busy with his job as personnel director at the Bank of England, still found time to ring me every day to see how I was doing, and give me a piece of advice!

For the second time, Crawley top-scored in each innings of the Varsity Match in 1993, but it was not enough to prevent the follow-on after Oxford had run up 400. Only a lively last-wicket stand of 70, another Cambridge match record, between Zimbabwe's Andrew Whittall and Croydon's Chris Pitcher, gave Oxford anything to chase, and an easy nine-wicket victory was duly completed. Faced with an eerily similar scenario in 1994, Whittall, now captain, twice rescued his side from a drastic situation. In the first innings, he marshalled the tail to such effect that Cambridge recovered from 94 for six to 253 all out. Following on again, the score was 105 for six when the skipper came in, and he now played the innings of his life, a scintillating 91 not out that left Oxford in despair and let Cambridge off the hook.

Professor David Buckingham CBE, current President of the Club.

Whittall was captain again in 1995, when Russell Cake, who had first come to notice in 1993 with a hundred for the Combined Universities against Australia, scored over 500 runs with an average of 46. He also obtained a starred First in his final engineering exams, one of several examples in the 1990s of an outstanding cricketer with real academic credentials, a fact still lost on admissions tutors. Whittall himself took eleven wickets against Essex, and in general there was a greater competitiveness than for many years. The exception was in the two Varsity Matches, both of which were lost all too easily. The first ever one-day Varsity Match was held at Fenner's, but home advantage meant nothing as Cambridge went down by 112 runs. Cake scored another hundred in the three-day game, and the Light Blues were in charge for the first half of the match. Although Cake again top-scored in the second innings, the tail did not wag this time after another collapse, and Oxford needed only 190 to win. Gregor Macmillan completed a nine-wicket win with two successive sixes into the Mound Stand, and Cambridge went off to lick its wounds once again.

The Fenner's pitches had finally been relaid in 1995 under the supervision of John Moden. Tony Pocock, who had taken over from Cyril Coote after the latter retired in 1979, had been forced to resign through illness the previous winter, although he later conducted an unsuccessful case against the University for constructive dismissal. David Hallett was full of praise for the new square, commenting on:

the vastly improved quality of the pitches after the Fenner's square was completely relaid… the first time around, they produced pace and evenness of bounce not evident for years.

The pitch being relaid in the mid-1990s.

Three young batsmen had reason to be particularly grateful for this return to the days of old, especially as they now had the irrepressible Derek Randall as coach. Ed Smith of Tonbridge was an immediate beneficiary, showing great application in his debut innings of 101 against Glamorgan in the first match of 1996. Will House, a left-hander from Sevenoaks, followed this in the second match with a stylish 136 off 123 balls, and Anurag Singh of King Edward's, Birmingham, weighed in with a century in the one-day Varsity Match, which Cambridge won for the first time. With each of this trio scoring over 500 runs, the batting was always competitive, but the inadequacies of the bowling were fully exposed against Oxford, who racked up a new match record of 513 for six declared. Ultimately set 413 to win, Cambridge comfortably played out time, but it was a disappointing end to a highly encouraging season.

It was Cambridge's turn to start as favourites in 1997, after a win in the one-day game, and an exceptional run of form by Smith, who finished the short university season heading the national averages with 683 runs at an average of 68. He failed twice in the Varsity Match, but his captain Singh scored 91, and House a dashing 94 off ninety balls. Steffan Jones, currently with Northamptonshire after several years at Somerset, gave his team every chance with six for 67, and Singh was able to set a target of 326 in around sixty overs. Jones took three more wickets, but at the end Oxford was just holding out on 249 for eight.

The old joke about snow stopping play became all too serious at the start of the 1998 season, as Cambridge suffered one of the most miserable springs in living memory. The snow fell at the start of the game against Northamptonshire, and the Derbyshire fixture was abandoned without a ball being bowled. Most disappointing of all for some was the curtailment of the celebrations marking 150 years at Fenner's, with neither of the two games planned reaching a conclusion. All this was a bitter pill to swallow for a team that contained some of the best batsmen since the 1950s, leading to high hopes being dashed.

Both Oxford and Cambridge felt under-prepared coming to Lord's, but at least Oxford finally had the chance to come into some form with a successful run-chase against Kent. Imraan Mohammed, son of the great Sadiq, had just scored a century against Yorkshire, but this was balanced for the Light Blues by an injury to Ed Smith, a leading light in 1997. The feeling was, however, that if Cambridge batted first then New Zealander Greg Loveridge's leg-breaks might be too much for the frail Oxford lower order on a last day pitch.

Oxford captain Jim Fulton gave this strategy a helping hand by putting Cambridge into bat, but its supporters would have been disappointed with a generally lacklustre display. The outstanding exception was captain Anurag Singh, who completed a sparkling hundred off 162 balls. All chance of a really good total vanished when he ran out the explosive Loveridge, whose arrival back in the changing room was accompanied by the inharmonious tinkling of glass.

Singh tried to make it up to Loveridge in the evening session by giving him the new ball after declaring just short of 300, but this adventurous move was not

Right: *The sun shone just long enough for Dickie Bird to cut the cake at Fenner's' 150th birthday.*

Below: *The Varsity Match 1998. Greg Loveridge is applauded from the field.*

matched by results. Oxford moved serenely on the next day, with Mark Wagh giving a particularly polished display, but just as the match began to drift, more innovation led to an agreement that Oxford would declare behind if Cambridge tried to set them a target of around 330. With his side 114 ahead, Singh again showed the way, and he and Will House added 70 at a run a minute, but a wholehearted effort from opening bowler David Mather prevented Cambridge from setting up quite as challenging target as they had wanted. Even so, 291 in eighty-four overs was quite a stiff task, and a lot depended on Wagh playing a major innings.

Oxford began slowly against accurate bowling from Adam Janisch, but Wagh started to raise the tempo. Once he fell, caught behind off the deserving Janisch, Oxford's hopes rested with Byrne and Claughton. With twenty-two overs left, the score stood at 186 for five – 105 needed. Loveridge now came into his own, starting a collapse by removing Claughton. With eight wickets down for 194, spectators were treated to the unedifying sight of Oxford coach Gary Palmer running onto the field to dispute the number of overs remaining after misreading the rule book. As it turned out, Loveridge needed only two more overs to complete the rout, and Cambridge took the honours for the first time since 1992. It was a fitting finale for the triumvirate that had done so much to keep Cambridge cricket afloat in the second half of the nineties, and for two of them at least it provided a launching-pad

The scorecard tells a happy story.

for a successful county career. House never quite made it after playing briefly for both Kent and Sussex, while Singh has had a peripatetic existence, moving from Warwickshire, via Worcestershire, to his current county Nottinghamshire. Smith, however, has been one of the best county batsmen of his generation, and in 2003 was in such prime form for Kent that he made three appearances for England against South Africa. It is possible that he will be the last Cambridge Blue to represent his country, but small miracles should never be discounted.

Events off the field were to prove just as significant as those on it in 1999, which was supremely unfair as Cambridge overall produced its best cricket of the decade. Despite the loss of its four most influential Blues, the team was competitive in every game except that against Kent, when it was severely depleted by injuries and academic demands. Otherwise, Quentin Hughes adopted a positive attitude as captain, which permeated the rest of the side. A promising seamer was unearthed in Samir Sheikh, and for once there were two all-rounders, South African Ken Walker and Richard Halsall. Greg Loveridge, who damaged ankle ligaments in the opening game, averaged 50 with the bat, making up for less success with the ball. All this came at a time when the English Cricket Board was finally announcing its decision on the future structure of the university game. The plan to set up six centres of excellence around the country naturally met with some misgivings, but the powers that be at Cambridge were sensible enough to realise that this could be the only way of retaining first-class cricket at Fenner's. This was to be the penultimate season as Cambridge University alone, as from 2001 the squad included players from Anglia Polytechnic University for the first time. Those lucky enough to wear the Light Blue in 1999 were determined to make the most of it.

Typically, Hughes decided to bat on winning the toss against Middlesex in the season's last game at Fenner's. Imraan was run out just as he was getting into his stride, but Loveridge thrashed 50 off sixty-nine balls, an excellent cure for his hangover from the previous night's May Ball. With Halsall using the slog drive to great effect, they added 103 in twenty-one overs for the fifth wicket, enabling Hughes to declare before the close, which Middlesex reached without loss. The next day the young Owais Shah reached a cultured century off 190 balls, but Nash was his only real support and Shah was content to declare ten runs behind. Hughes and Imraan made good progress up to stumps, which saw Cambridge 76 ahead with nine wickets intact. Hughes showed his dedication to the side above the individual by declaring with his friend James Pyemont 10 short of his maiden first-class hundred, leaving Middlesex needing an eminently gettable 252 in fifty-nine overs. A dramatic start to the innings was made into a regrettable incident when Kettleborough shouldered arms to a straight ball from Sheikh. He kicked the stumps twice as he left, the second time as umpire Reed was about to replace them. As if that was not enough, Andrew Strauss, England's hero of 2004, then pointed theatrically to his shoulder after being adjudged caught behind. The club later suspended Kettleborough and reprimanded Strauss, but Cambridge carried on unperturbed. At tea, Middlesex was 65 for seven, and although Hewitt struck a few judicious blows, the result was never in doubt. Nor was the fact that the more professional unit had won.

Cambridge in the field in 1999.

Cambridge came to Lord's as favourite to retain the crown, and at the end of the second day it was in a strong position to do just that. Imraan made 87, Pyemont was run out for another 90, and Hughes notched 101, creating a first-innings lead of 152. Oxford was poised at 43 for one overnight, but in the end a combination of rain, which prevented play for nearly two hours after lunch, and dropped catches, allowed it to escape. A crucial drop at 171 for six, with Oxford only 19 ahead and sixteen overs left, was the turning point, and after that no further inroads could be made; seven overs were left when Hughes conceded the draw. James Pyemont became the last captain of Cambridge University against a county side in 2000, and led the team out at Lord's for the final three-day Varsity Match at Lord's, which ended in anti-climax as a very damp draw. Hughes and Pyemont again batted majestically when time allowed, both scoring centuries as they set up a new match third-wicket record of 187. No play was possible on the third day, and so, sadly, a long and glorious association came to an end. Fittingly, exactly 150 matches had been played at the game's headquarters; Cambridge had won fifty-five, Oxford forty-four, and fifty-one had been drawn. If only Cambridge could be in the same position after another 150 games.

FIFTEEN

WHAT OF THE FUTURE?

In 2001, as part of the deal for the future of cricket in Cambridge, the University team became Cambridge University Centre of Cricketing Excellence, and the only match allowed at Lord's was the one-day Varsity Match, although there was some compensation in the fact that all those who played in this game were henceforth awarded a Blue. However, the University Match proper retained its first-class status, and was granted four days to bring it in line with county cricket. This was now the only first-class match played by Oxford and Cambridge Universities, as the three matches against the counties were subsequently to be under the banner of UCCE.

David Hallett, for one, was sceptical as to whether Cambridge University Cricket Club would derive much benefit from the scheme:

The advent of a cricket school to which students must offer commitment is hardly likely to encourage Cambridge admission tutors to welcome a new breed of cricketing undergraduate... at least two applicants with all the necessary academic entry requirements were rejected, only to be quickly offered places at other universities.

Sure enough, the first year of the new regime coincided with a dearth in talent, and as APU was yet to recruit any high-class cricketers, it was left to CUCC to fill the breach. It provided all the players for each of the three county games, and the lack of depth was shown up in a colossal defeat by Essex. The other two games were drawn due to the weather, but only Stuart Block showed much application, living up to his name by carrying his bat against Kent, scoring 56 in seventy-seven overs. The University was in charge of the Varsity Match when it had Oxford 203 for seven in reply to its 296, but the Dark Blues recovered to 325 all out, Floyd carrying his bat for 128. Cambridge managed to set a target of 205 in sixty-nine overs, but without a proper spinner the game slipped away, and Oxford eased home by three wickets with six overs to spare.

Changing times in 2001.

There was not much to choose between the ancient combatants in 2002, but Oxford was buoyed by its win in the Lord's one-day game as the sides travelled to The Parks. Faced with a typically placid pitch, Jamie Parker, son of Paul, had no trouble deciding to take first strike, and after two early alarms, the captain and Adrian Shankar set about exacting their revenge. After they had put on 180 for the third wicket, Stuart Moffat, in his first and probably only first-class game, added a further 159 with Shankar, before the latter departed just before the close, with Moffat poised on 96 out of Cambridge's 389 for five. Moffat, on the verge of joining Glasgow Caledonians as a professional rugby player, set about dismembering the Oxford attack the next day, finishing with seventeen fours and five sixes in his 193-ball innings. Sensibly, he was content to leave first-class cricket with an average of 169, and Cambridge, with a total of 604, could also be happy with the highest score by either side in 175 years of the fixture. Oxford followed-on after a tight bowling display by Cambridge, but even four days was not enough to force a result on this wicket, Jamie Dalrymple of Middlesex steering them to safety on the last day.

Chris Scott, former Nottinghamshire and Durham wicketkeeper, had been appointed to succeed the ever-popular Derek Randall as coach at the start of 2001. Despite the first two seasons showing few signs of progress, he remained optimistic about the future of the UCCE scheme:

The scoreboard shows Cambridge's record total in 2002.

Chris Scott in front of the 1970s pavilion.

Simon Marshall reaches his hundred: Fenner's 2003.

I believe that significant improvement will only be seen over a five-year period, and feel that the signs are already there in this year's squad. We have a lad in his first year at Pembroke College (Simon Marshall) who scored 99 against Essex. They were so impressed that they asked him to join their second eleven. This year's performances have been an improvement on last year, and we have some very good freshers coming next year. The provision of a purpose-built indoor cricket school, provided our National Lottery bid is successful, will make a tremendous difference.

Scott's confidence, both in Marshall and the UCCE set-up, was seen to be justified sooner than even he could have expected. In 2003, Marshall captained the side, now made up of a roughly equal number of players from both universities, to a pulsating win against Northamptonshire, the first against a county by any of the Centres of Excellence since its inception. Although most of the run-chase was dominated by APU batsmen, Marshall himself scored a vital and timely 50, and later proved his worth once again in the Varsity Match, held at Fenner's for the second time. Oxford's Jamie Dalrymple dominated the match from start to finish, first setting a new third-wicket record stand of 263, before declaring on a new Oxford match best of 522 for seven. He seemed blissfully unaware that his personal tally of 236 not out was just two short of the Nawab of Pataudi's record, but to be fair the standard of the Cambridge attack was far short of what it had been in 1931, and so it seemed fitting that his mark should not be overtaken. Dalrymple soon consoled himself with a five-wicket haul as Oxford's spin triplets got to work. Following on with nothing more than a draw to hope for, Cambridge showed a little more application, but only

Marshall had the ability to survive for long. Left stranded on 126 not out, he could not prevent an innings defeat, giving Oxford a 100 per cent record at Fenner's.

In 2004, he once again demonstrated the talent that meant he was the most likely of his era to make a successful transition to county cricket. Except for the fact that Cambridge batted first, the Varsity Match followed a remarkably similar pattern to the previous year, with Cambridge collapsing twice to the spinners in the face of a substantial Oxford total. Only Marshall stood firm in the first innings, scoring an exemplary 98 out of a paltry 174, and in the second he and Shankar, Club captain for the second year in a row, looked in no trouble at all until he was run out. There was no way back from there, and the Light Blues went down to their second successive innings defeat, the first time this had happened in the fixture since 1853. Cambridge was struggling to show its old Lord's form, having lost three of the four games since the move from St John's Wood. It was clear that Marshall's colleagues needed to take a leaf from his book, raising their game for the big occasion in a way that seemed second nature to Oxford. Marshall's departure at the end of the season left a big hole, but at least he had a fair chance of establishing a solid career with Lancashire.

What of the future for Cambridge University Cricket Club? Clearly, as senior treasurer Ken Siddle has pointed out:

While the raison d'etre of CUCC must always be to provide the best possible playing opportunities and cricketing fellowship for Cambridge students, we recognise our total dependence on external financial support and our obligation to earn this support by contributing to the wider development of the game both locally and nationally.

Can the Club continue to do that, when academic pressures are so great, and the only first-class game played now is against Oxford, another team whose status seems increasingly absurd on the face of it? This was rammed home further than ever in 2004, when, to the dismay of many members, APU contributed many more players to the UCCE squad. Will the Club maintain its standing if this is a sign of things to come?

I contend that it can and will continue to make a contribution to the development of the game, and retain the respect of the authorities, but it must get the full backing of the University for this to happen. Those, like David Hallett, who have followed the Club's fortunes for many years, believe that this will come, although it may need a real financial crisis before positive action is finally taken. It must not let the priceless asset that is Fenner's go to waste, especially now it has been enhanced by the opening of the new cricket school. As an institution that is committed to excellence in all things, it would be extremely short-sighted if the University did not fight to keep the highest possible standard of cricket; if it is achievable in rowing and rugby, why not in a sport that is at least as popular as either of them?

The Club is beginning to play its part, particularly through encouraging women's cricket throughout the University, and by launching energetic marketing campaigns, targeted particularly at old Blues. There is still room for imaginative ways of reviving interest in the Varsity Match, one of which has been put forward by our old friend Mr Hallett:

I was in favour of a move away from Lord's before they did. I thought somewhere like Arundel would be appropriate. They could really make something of it with a whole week's festival and it would generate some money because there would be something to focus on.

In the haste to emphasise the Club's role as a nursery for the game at large, we should not forget the precious traditional fixtures, neglected by the spectator, but still its lifeblood; matches against Quidnuncs, Free Foresters, MCC and the Duke of Norfolk's XI that are still played in a positive and entertaining manner. It is perhaps these 'friendly' games that give a clue to what will be the greatest contribution of the Club to the future of cricket. This will be, as it always has, the nurturing of attacking cricketers who play the game in the way that nature intended; who represent, in Lord Cowdrey's felicitous phrase, the true 'spirit of cricket'. And if a few more England captains are produced on the way, so much the better.

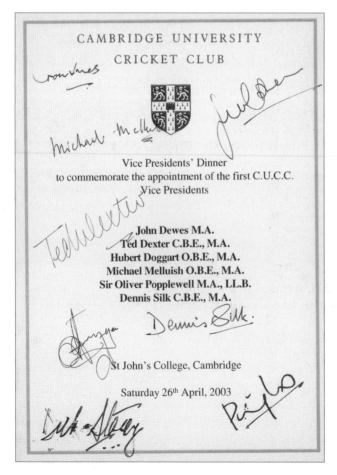

Six Vice-Presidents of the Club were inducted at a special dinner in 2003.

CAMBRIDGE UNIVERSITY CRICKET CLUB RECORDS TO THE END OF THE 2004 SEASON

TEAM

Highest Total:
For: 703 for nine declared *v.* Sussex, Hove 1890
Against: 730 for three *v.* West Indies, Fenner's 1950
Lowest Total:
For: 30 *v.* Yorkshire, Fenner's 1928
Against: 32 *v.* Oxford, Lord's 1878

BATTING

Highest Innings:
For: 254★ K.S. Duleepsinhji, Fenner's 1927
Against: 304★ E.de C. Weekes, Fenner's 1950
Most Runs in a Season: 1,581, average 79.05 D.S. Sheppard 1952
Most Hundreds in a Season: 7 D.S. Sheppard 1952
Most Runs in a Career : 4,310, average 38.48 J.M. Brearley 1961–8
Most Hundreds in a Career: 14 D.S. Sheppard 1950–2

BOWLING

Most Wickets in a Season: 80, average 17.63 O.S. Wheatley 1958
Most Wickets in a Career: 208, average 21.82 G. Goonesena 1954–7
Best Bowling in an Innings: For: 10-69 S.M.J. Woods *v.* C.I. Thornton's XI, Fenner's 1890
Against: 10-38 S.E. Butler, *v.* Oxford, Lord's 1871
Best Bowling in a Match:
For: 15-88 S.M.J. Woods *v.* C.I. Thornton's XI, Fenner's 1890
Against: 15-95 S.E. Butler, *v.* Oxford, Lord's 1871

PARTNERSHIPS

1st	349	J.G. Dewes and D.S. Sheppard *v.* Sussex, Hove 1950
2nd	429★	J.G. Dewes and G.H.G. Doggart *v.* Essex, Fenner's 1949
3rd	284	E.T. Killick and G.C. Grant *v.* Essex, Fenner's 1929
4th	275	R. de W.K. Winlaw and J.H. Human *v.* Essex, Fenner's 1934
5th	220	R. Subba Row and F.C.M. Alexander *v.* Nottinghamshire, Nottingham 1953
6th	245	J.L. Bryan and C.T. Ashton *v.* Surrey, The Oval 1921
7th	289	G. Goonesena and G.W. Cook *v.* Oxford, Lord's 1957
8th	145	H. Ashton and A.E.R. Gilligan *v.* Free Foresters, Fenner's 1920
9th	200	G.W. Cook and C.S. Smith *v.* Lancashire, Liverpool 1957
10th	177	A.E.R. Gilligan and J.H. Naumann *v.* Sussex, Hove 1919

BIBLIOGRAPHY

BOOKS

Allen, D.R. *Sir Aubrey* (Elm Tree Books 1982)

Atherton, M.A. *Opening Up* (Hodder & Stoughton 2002)

Bailey, P. and Thorn, P. *Cambridge University Cricketers 1820–1992* (Association of Cricket Statisticians & Historians 1992)

Betham, J.D. *Oxford and Cambridge Scores and Biographies* (Simpkin, Marshall 1905)

Bolton, G. *History of the Oxford University Cricket Club* (Holywell Press 1962)

Cambridge University Cricket Club. *Fenner's '83* (CUCC 1983)

Chesterton, G.H. and Doggart, G.H.G. *Oxford and Cambridge Cricket* (Collins Willow 1989)

Coldham, J.P. *F.S. Jackson* (Crowood Press 1989)

Croome, A.C.M. (ed.) *Fifty Years of Sport at Oxford, Cambridge and the Great Public Schools* (Southwood 1913)

Dexter, E.R. *Ted Dexter Declares* (Stanley Paul 1966)

Dodd, C. *The Oxford and Cambridge Boat Race* (Stanley Paul 1983)

Farnes, K. *Tours and Tests* (Lutterworth 1940)

Foley, C.P. *Autumn Foliage* (Methuen 1935)

Foot, D. *Cricket's Unholy Trinity* (Stanley Paul 1985)

Ford, W.J. *The Cambridge University Cricket Club 1820–1901* (Blackwood 1902)

Frindall, W.H. *The Wisden Book of Cricket Records – 4th edition* (Headline 1998)

Glover, W. *The Memoirs of a Cambridge Chorister* (Hurst and Blackett 1885)

Grant, G.C. *Jack Grant's Story* (Lutterworth 1980)

Gray, A. and Brittain, F. *A History of Jesus College Cambridge* (Heinemann 1960)

Grayson, E. *Corinthians and Cricketers* (Naldrett Press 1955)

Grubb, N.P. *C.T. Studd Cricketer and Pioneer* (Lutterworth 1933)

Hargreaves-Maudsley, W.N. (ed.) *Woodforde at Oxford 1759–1776* (Clarendon Press 1967–8)

Hawke, Lord. *Recollections and Reminiscences* (Williams and Norgate 1924)

Huber, V.A. *The English Universities* (Pickering 1843)

Insole, D.J. *Cricket From the Middle* (Heinemann 1960)

Jessop, G.L. *A Cricketer's Log* (Hodder & Stoughton 1922)

Johnson, R.B. (ed.) *Social Life at the English Universities in the Eighteenth Century* (Stanley Paul 1928)

Lewis, A.R. *Playing Days* (Stanley Paul 1985)

Lyttelton, E. *Alfred Lyttelton: an account of his life* (Longman 1917)

Meredith, A. *The Demon and the Lobster* (Kingswood Press 1987)

Midwinter, E. *The Lost Seasons: Cricket in Wartime 1939–45* (Methuen 1987)

Piggott, P. *Fenner's: Reminiscences of Cambridge University Cricket –2nd edition* (Self-Published 1948)

Powell, W.A. *Varsity Cricket* (Tempus 2001)

Pullin, A.W. *Talks With Old English Cricketers* (Blackwood 1900)

Pycroft, J. *Oxford Memories* (Bentley 1886)

Ranjitsinhji, K.S. *The Jubilee Book of Cricket* (Blackwood 1897)

Robertson-Glasgow, R.C. *46 Not Out* (Hollis & Carter 1948)

Roget, J.L. *Cambridge Scrapbook* (Macmillan 1859)

Sewell, E.H.D. *Who's Won the Toss?* (Stanley Paul 1943)

Sheppard, D.S. *Parson's Pitch* (Hodder & Stoughton 1964)

Simons, G. *William Yardley – Master of Bat and Burlesque* (Wisteria 1997)

Standing, P.C. *Cricket of To-day and Yesterday* (Jack 1902)

Steel, A.G and Lyttelton, R.H. *Cricket* (Badminton Library 1888)

Swanton, E.W. *Gubby Allen – Man of Cricket* (Hutchinson 1985)

Venn, H. *The Letters of Henry Venn* (Banner of Truth Trust 1993)

Ward, G.R.M. *Oxford University Statutes Vol. 1* (Pickering 1845)

Wilde, S. *Ranji: a Genius Rich and Strange* (Kingswood Press 1991)

Wilson, F.B. *Sporting Pie* (Chapman and Hall 1922)

Woods, S.M.J. *My Reminiscences* (Chapman and Hall 1925)

Wordsworth, C. *Annals of My Early Life* (1891)

Yardley, N.W.D. *Cricket Campaigns* (Stanley Paul 1949)

PERIODICALS

Bell's Life in London and *Sporting Chronicle*

Cambridge Chronicle

Cambridge Evening News and its predecessors

Cambridge Independent Press

Cricket: A Weekly Record of the Game

The Cricketer

James Lillywhite's Cricketers' Annual

John Lillywhite's Cricketer's Companion

Lillywhite, F. (ed.): *The Guide to Cricketers*

Public Advertiser

The Times

Wisden Cricketers' Almanack

INDEX

Other titles published by Tempus

Victory England's Greatest Modern Test Wins
ALAN BONE WITH COMMENTARY BY CHRISTOPHER MARTIN-JENKINS

With a foreword and commentary from the inimitable Christopher Martin-Jenkins and a wealth of illustration, this book highlights the most memorable occasions on which England has triumphed, be it a consummate thrashing of the opposition or an epic against-all-odds comeback from the brink of defeat. This is a source of great nostalgia and delight for all England cricket fans.

0 7524 3415 2

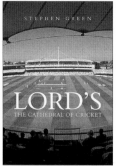

Lord's The Cathedral of Cricket
STEPHEN GREEN

Containing over 150 illustrations, this book follows the history of the ground from its foundation right up to the present day. Including visits by royalty, the construction of the Media Stand and countless great occasions in domestic and international cricket, it is sure to appeal to anyone who has an interest in the game. This is the story of the ground, the MCC – and of cricket itself.

0 7524 2167 0

Summer of '64 A Season in English Cricket
ANDREW HIGNELL

The halcyon summer of 1964 saw Graveney, Boycott and Wilson all make over 2,000 runs, while Shackleton, Harman, Cartwright, Titmus and Illingworth were the most lethal exponents of the art of bowling. After one of the hardest fought contests in living memory Australia very narrowly took the Ashes, while Worcestershire finally saw off intense competition to narrowly take the County Championship. An affectionate and nostalgic look at one of the finest seasons on record.

0 7524 3404 7

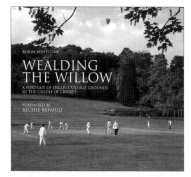

Wealding the Willow A Portrait of English Village Grounds in the Cradle of Cricket
ROBIN WHITCOMB

The Weald area of South East England has been known as 'the cradle of cricket', being the place where the game first started, and in many communities there the cricket ground is still at the very centre of village life. With a foreword by the much-loved cricket commentator Richie Benaud, this is a beautifully illustrated record of the great game and the places where it all began.

0 7524 3457 8

If you are interested in purchasing other books published by Tempus, or in case you have difficulty finding any Tempus books in your local bookshop, you can also place orders directly through our website
www.tempus-publishing.com